How To Teach

Backstroke

Basic technique drills, step-by-step lesson plans and everything in-between

A swimming teacher's definitive guide to teaching backstroke swimming stroke

Mark Young

A Catalogue record for this book is available from the British Library

ISBN 9780995484245

Published by: Educate & Learn Publishing, Hertfordshire, UK

Graphics by Mark Young, courtesy of Poser V6.0

Design and typeset by Mark Young

Published in association with www.swim-teach.com

Note: This book is intended for guidance and support only. The material contained here should accompany additional course material set on an official swimming teaching course by an official Swimming Association. Neither the author nor the publisher can accept responsibility for any injury or loss sustained as a result of the use of this material.

Author Online!
For more resources and swimming help visit
Mark Young's website at

www.swim-teach.com

Mark Young is a well-established swimming instructor with decades of experience of teaching thousands of adults and children to swim. He has taken nervous, frightened children and adults with a fear of water and made them happy and confident swimmers. He has also turned many of average ability into advanced swimmers. This book draws on his experiences and countless successes to put together this simplistic methodical approach to teaching swimming.

Also by Mark Young

Teaching Guides
How To Be A Swimming Teacher
101 Swimming Lesson Plans
How To Teach Front Crawl
How To Teach Breaststroke
How To Teach Butterfly

Learn to Swim Guides
The Complete Beginners Guide to Swimming
How To Swim Front Crawl
How To Swim Breaststroke
How To Swim Backstroke
How To Swim Butterfly
The Swimming Strokes Book

Contents

Introduction

Backstroke is the most efficient swimming stroke that a person can swim in a supine position. The alternating arm action provides the power, and the leg action balances the stroke. Achieving a flat body position is essential, and many pupils find this part the most difficult. Teaching backstroke can be challenging as many beginners find swimming on their back daunting.

What Makes A Good Teacher?

'A teacher is one who makes himself progressively unnecessary.'
Thomas Carruthers

What makes a good teacher?

A teacher is looked up to by their pupils as a role model and a source of knowledge and guidance. A teacher possesses several key characteristics that make him or her individual and it is these personal characteristics that can determine a teacher's level of success.

A good swimming teacher requires a wide range of qualities. You will probably be stronger in some areas than others and as you gain experience you will build your competence in all areas.

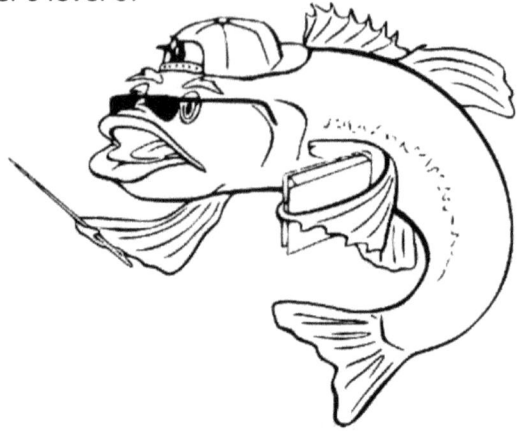

Teaching Qualities

To be a good teacher and role model to your pupils, you need to possess some essential qualities. These are:

Knowledge

Having sound knowledge of your subject gains you respect, not only from your pupils but from parents and other swimming teachers. You will need to keep your knowledge up to date and always admit when you don't know the answer, but make it your business to find out.

Empathy

Teaching swimming requires empathy on all levels. For example, the child who is scared and has every reason to be, the adult who is equally scared or even embarrassed, the child who is over-excited at the prospect of going in the pool and the child who is trying hard but not keeping up with the rest.

Patience

All of the above examples that require empathy will also test your patience. As a teacher, you have to accept that not everybody learns at the same rate. Children's behaviour and attention spans will also try your patience at times. Whatever is thrown at you, you must show patience and control at all times.

Control and Management

It goes without saying that you must have control over your class, especially with children in a pool. In the classroom at school, children know what is expected of them but this is not always the case in the swimming pool. Children have to be controlled for safety purposes as well as learning purposes.

If pupils are being unruly throughout the lesson then not only is the lesson unsafe, but they are not learning anything. The golden rule is to set out your stall early on to show them who is boss. That is not to say that you have to 'rule with fear', otherwise pupils will not want to have swimming lessons with you, just let those that step out of line know they have done so and that it will not be tolerated.

Effective Communication

As a teacher, your job is to pass on information effectively and clearly, and your ability to do this will determine how quickly your pupils learn. Knowledge of your subject is also essential, but how you convey that knowledge is far more important. You could be a world expert on the human body and the scientific principles behind swimming but if you are not able to pass that expertise onto eager-to- learn pupils clearly and concisely, then you are not a good teacher!

Basic Principles of Effective Communication

Positioning

Where you position yourself on the poolside will determine how well your pupils can see and hear you. Study the pool diagrams in the planning and organisation section for best practice.

Clarity

Passing information on clearly will ensure your pupils do exactly what you want them to.

Conciseness

Keep your teaching concise to avoid your pupils becoming confused or taking in the wrong pieces of information.

Accuracy

Your teaching has to be accurate as you will be copied, mimicked and quoted especially by children. Inaccuracy will result in your pupils not learning and in you gaining a reputation as a poor teacher.

Enthusiasm

A sure way to motivate your class and get results is to have an enthusiastic approach. Enthusiasm is infectious and if you are full of it when you teach, your pupils will put every effort into what you ask them to do.

Interest

If the content of what you teach is not interesting then your pupils will not listen and become distracted. Enthusiasm and interesting content go hand in hand, as one breeds the other. The most uninteresting subject can be made interesting with an injection of enthusiasm.

Appropriateness

The teaching points and practices you use will determine the success and outcome of the lesson. If your methods are not appropriate, the pupils do not learn and the lesson becomes pointless.

Two-way

Communication works both ways. Ask your pupils questions and listen carefully to those who answer and how they answer. Encourage them to ask you questions at appropriate times.

Motivation

As a teacher, you are also a motivator. Some pupils you teach will need more motivation than others. Most children can't wait to get into the pool and start swimming and impress the teacher.

You will, however, come across children who have swimming lessons because they have been made to do so by their parents, whether they need them or not. Either way, a motivating teacher brings out the best in pupils.

Praise

This is the easiest, most common form of motivation. Remember to praise effort as well as success.

Feedback

This is a more detailed, constructive form of praise. The pupils are given a clearer picture of how they are performing and improving. If feedback is to be motivational it has to be positive.

For example, a swimmer returns to the poolside after practising backstroke leg kick unsuccessfully. Your job is to teach and motivate them. Your feedback should go something like this:

'Well done, that was a good try' (praise for the effort)
'You were pointing your toes, which is good, well done.' (positive feedback)
'Try again, and this time kick your legs from your hips.' (feedback in the form of a teaching point)
Avoid negative feedback, for example, *'Don't bend your legs.'*

Teaching Adults

Adults will arrive on the poolside in all shapes and sizes and with differing levels of confidence. One thing that they will all have in common, however, is that they will all appreciate a relaxed and informal approach to being taught to swim.

Most adults will need some intervention when learning to swim on their back. Learning to swim in a supine position will test their confidence, ability to float and awareness of their surroundings.

Teaching adults how to swim backstroke does bring some common barriers and limitations. These include:

Lack of Flexibility

Generally speaking, adults lack flexibility all over, so when it comes to swimming backstroke, the main area that requires a significant degree of movement is the shoulders. As a result, their arm action can often be limited. Arm pulls might be shortened due to their inability to stretch up fully so that the arm brushes past the ear. Adult backstroke arms often enter the water at an angle, wide of the body line.

The other area where adults often lack flexibility is in their ankles, which can affect the leg kick by preventing the feet and toes from pointing as they kick. The lack of ankle movement can make the overall kick inefficient and cause drag. A lack of movement in the ankles also means losing the relaxed flipper-like action as they kick. This lack of flexibility can result in either an excessive knee bend as they kick or their feet and legs gradually sinking, compromising the overall body position.

These lack of flexibilities often make for a very inefficient swimming stroke.

Lack of Confidence

When learning to swim front crawl, breaststroke or any other method on the front, swimmers can see where they are going, and they can see the water surface, the poolside and the pool floor. In short, they have total awareness of where they are and what they are doing. This awareness and perception is removed when learning to swim on the back, which significantly affects confidence.

Add together these two most common limitations and you have what most swimming teachers experience when teaching adults to swim - very slow progress.

Slow progress in adults learning to swim is completely normal and should not be looked upon negatively.

As a swimming teacher, there are a few things you can do to help.

- Be calm, relaxed and informal in your teaching style. This will help to relax your adult and keep them at ease.
- Adjust your expectations accordingly.
- Take their limitations into account when planning. Exercises and drills that suit one swimmer may not work for another.
- Be flexible in your approach. For example, fins or hand paddles (usually used in advanced drills) can often be beneficial to adult beginners, as long as they do not become reliant on them.
- Be sensitive to their frustrations and always show empathy and be supportive in your response.
- Above all, use plenty of praise to stimulate and maintain motivation. At the end of each lesson, pick out the parts they showed progress and highlight them as achievements of the session however small they may be.

Equipment

Equipment

Floats and kickboards

When used correctly swimming floats can help develop specific parts of your technique. They are suitable for non-swimmers right up to advanced swimmers and can be used by both adults and children.

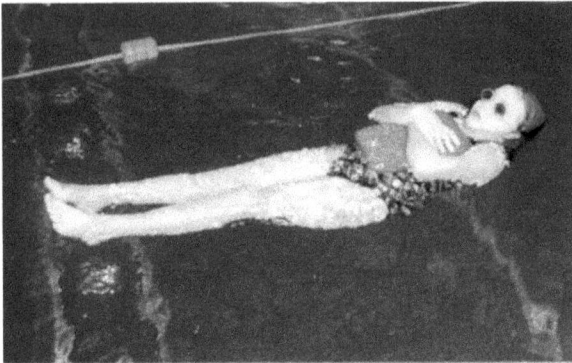

Swim floats are used by swimming teachers as part of lessons for many different exercises. They can be used by non-swimmers to strengthen and by established swimmers to isolate and perfect technique.

For example, the weak non-swimmer can use two floats, one placed under each arm, to help encourage a flat body position whilst practicing the leg kick. The floats will provide stability and help boost confidence, whilst encouraging a relaxed and steady leg kick.

Advantages:
- Very versatile and can help enhance a wide range of swimming exercises.
- Can be used in addition to other aids.
- Can be used in place of other types of swimming aid to encourage progression and enhance strength and stamina.
- When used individually floats can help gain leg or arm strength.
- Fine-tune technique by encouraging a swimmer to focus on a certain area of their swimming stroke.
- Cheap to buy and easy to store. Also easy to use with large groups.

Disadvantages:

- Not suitable for very young children or babies learning to swim as they require a degree of strength to hold.
- Require close supervision

Common Mistakes to Watch Out For

It's difficult to use a float incorrectly because they are such a simple piece of swimming equipment. However, there are a couple of points to watch out for when using floats to teach children.

Firstly, it is common for children to grip the float too tightly, especially if they are a nervous beginner. They squeeze the float in their hand, resulting in a very tired hand grip and the focus away from the part of their swimming they are supposed to be concentrating on.

Secondly, it is common for children to bare their weight onto the float, causing it to submerge. Once again this is easily done by the nervous beginner as they attempt to climb above the water surface instead of laying on the surface. Reassuring them and helping them to relax by advising them to "let the float support you", will go some way to helping children to get the most out of swimming floats.

These common problems can take time to fix as the swimmer begins to learn how to relax and become comfortable in the water. As long as the teacher is aware and the swimmer is made aware, then gradual progress can be made.

Woggle or Noodle

One of the most popular buoyancy aids, the swimming noodle, is a simple polythene foam cylinder. One of the most popular and widely used floats during swimming lessons.

Sometimes called a 'woggle', it is cheap to make, cheap to buy and easy to use in large group swimming lessons.

The main advantage is that it provides a high level of support whilst at the same time allowing the swimmer movement of their arms and legs. The swimmer can learn and experience propulsion through the water from both the arms and the legs.

The noodle is very versatile and as it is not a fixed aid, it can be used and removed with ease. It can also add a sense of fun to swimming as it can be tucked under the arms on the front and the back as well as placed between the legs and used as a 'horse'. The noodle is ideal for beginners learning backstroke body position and kicking technique.

Advantages and Disadvantages of a Swimming Noodle

Advantages:

- Provides a high level of support for children of all sizes.
- Gives a sense of independence in the water with the minimum of support.

- Allows freedom of movement.
- Boosts confidence in the nervous beginner.
- Able to support adult beginners
- Easy to fit and remove, so ideal for use in group swimming lessons.
- Allows freedom of movement.

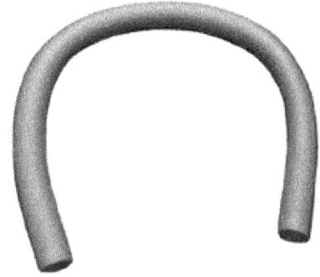

Disadvantages:

- Limited or no use for advanced swimmers.
- Nervous swimmers can 'clamp' it between their body and their arms, restricting their movements.

Pull Buoy

A pull buoy is a figure-eight shaped piece of solid foam and used mainly by established and advanced swimmers.

It is placed between the legs in the upper thigh area to provide support to the body so the swimmer can swim without kicking the legs. This allows them to focus on other parts of their swimming stroke, such as arm technique or breathing technique.

This type of swimming aid is most useful when learning and practising front crawl and backstroke techniques.

These training aids are most commonly used by competitive swimmers during their training sessions. They are designed to restrict the use of the swimmer's lower body, causing a greater intensity on the arms and upper body.

The nature of holding it between the legs by squeezing the thighs together also helps to keep the lower body in a streamlined and efficient shape during the swim.

By isolating the upper body, the swimmer can focus completely on their arm or breathing technique, whilst the float assists to keep the lower body afloat.

They also help to strengthen the upper body and arms by eliminating the kick propulsion, while helping to keep the body position correct in the water.

This type of swimming aid is available in a smaller size for younger swimmers as well as full size for adults.

Pull Buoy Advantages and Disadvantages

Advantages:

- Provide good isolation of the upper body whilst keeping the lower body buoyant.
- Ideal for work-outs and training and therefore for established and advanced swimmers.
- Increased core strength
- Available in adult and junior sizes

Disadvantages:

- Not suitable for non-swimmers and beginners.

Sinkers

Sinkers are objects such as sticks, hoops and toys that sink to
the bottom of the pool. They are a
great way to teach children breath control by
encouraging them to submerge.

Sinkers can be used in both shallow and deep
water and vary in design to cater for a range of
ages. Although their uses rarely target a
specific swimming stroke, they can open up a
huge range of contrasting and complementary
activities.

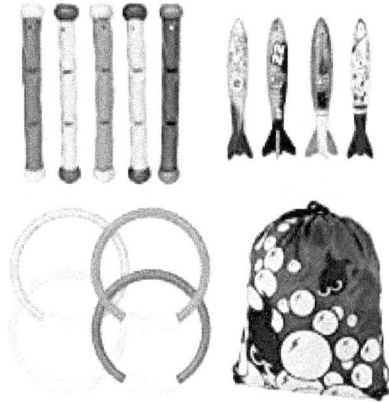

To children, sinkers are the equivalent of toys, so a swimming teacher with a
creative imagination can use them to spark excitement and get some fantastic
results.

Hand Paddles

Hand paddles can be used to develop power in the arms,
chest, shoulders and back muscles.
They come in the form of large plastic paddles
that strap to the palms of the hands and prevent
the water from passing through the fingers.

The swimmer can use hand paddles to enhance
their feel for the water and in that, in turn, will
help to improve technique.

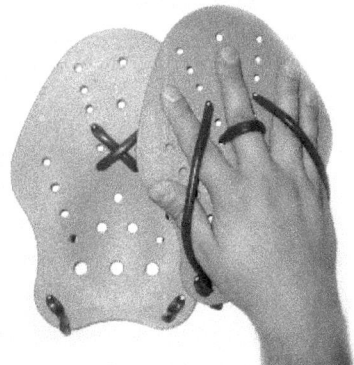

Backstroke Technique

Backstroke Technique

Backstroke is the most efficient stroke swum on the back and is the third fastest of all swimming strokes. The alternating arm technique produces most of the power, and its horizontal streamlined body position gives it its efficiency. Therefore this is the preferred stroke in competitive races swum on the back.

The nature of floating on the back and face-up (supine) can be a calming and relaxing feeling. Also, the face is clear of the water, allowing easy breathing and little water splashes onto the face. On the other hand, it can be counter-productive at first. It can give a feeling of disorientation and unease, as the swimmer is facing upwards and unaware of their surroundings.

The prone body position is flat and horizontal, with ears slightly below the water surface. The legs kick in an alternating action, continuously up and down, to help balance the movement of the arms. This stroke has two different arm actions: the bent arm pull, which is the most efficient, and the straight arm pull, which is the easiest to learn. Therefore the straight arm pull is best for beginners.

Breathing should be in time with the recovery of each arm, breathing in with one arm recovery and out with the other. Ideally, there should be 6 leg kicks to one arm cycle, but the stroke timing may vary according to the swimmer's level of coordination.

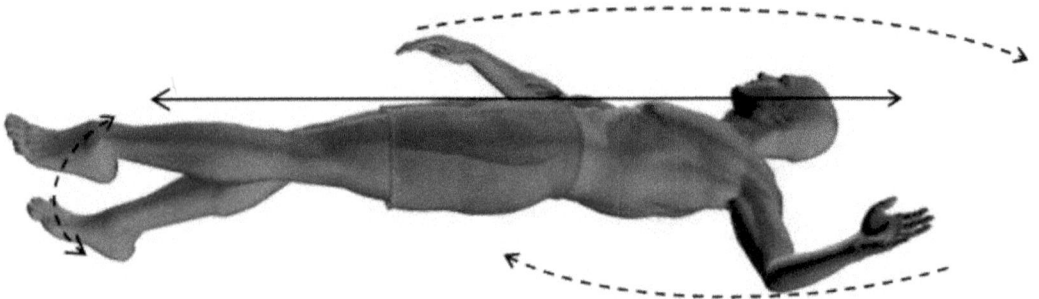

Body Position

The supine body position for this stroke is flat and horizontal, with ears slightly below the water surface.

Good floaters will find this position relaxing and relatively easy. In contrast, poor floaters will find it challenging to achieve a comfortable head position.

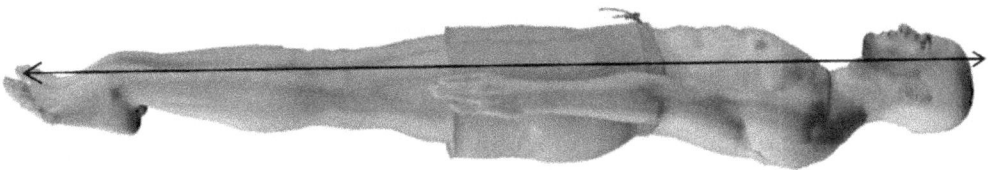

Body position remains horizontal and relaxed

The head remains still throughout the stroke. The eyes look slightly down the body, looking at a point the swimmer is swimming away from.

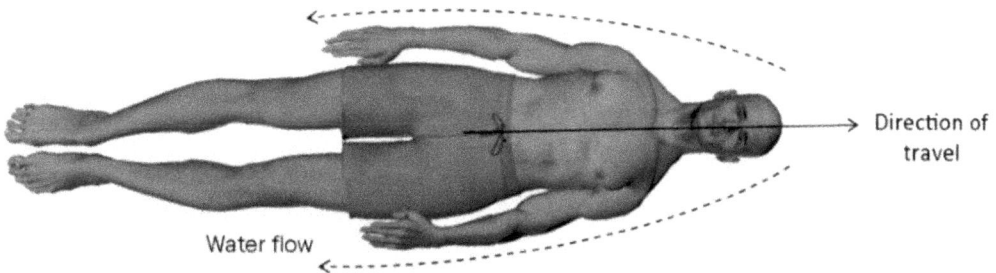

The head position is essential because a raised head makes it more challenging to keep the hips raised in the correct position, leading to a sitting position in the water. The hips and shoulders remain at or near the water surface but roll with the stroke. The legs and feet should be extended and stay together to maximise efficiency, with knees below the water surface.

Common body position mistakes

It is common to allow the legs to drop and the body position to become angled in the water without knowing it is happening. This is usually caused either by allowing the hips to fall or lifting the head slightly, or a combination of both. The whole stroke becomes less efficient and more energy-consuming as the legs drop deeper.

Performing a push and glide from holding the poolside is a good way of testing how flat you can remain. Ensure that you look upwards as you push away and stretch out so that your hips, legs and feet rise to the surface. Maintaining an overall body position is easier with a correct and efficient leg kick.

Leg Kick

The legs kick in an alternating action, continuously up and down, to help balance the movement of the arms.

The swimmer's legs should be stretched out with toes pointed (plantar flexed), and ankles should be relaxed and loose with toes pointing slightly inwards. The amount of propulsion generated from the kick will depend on the size of the feet, ankle mobility and strength of the legs.

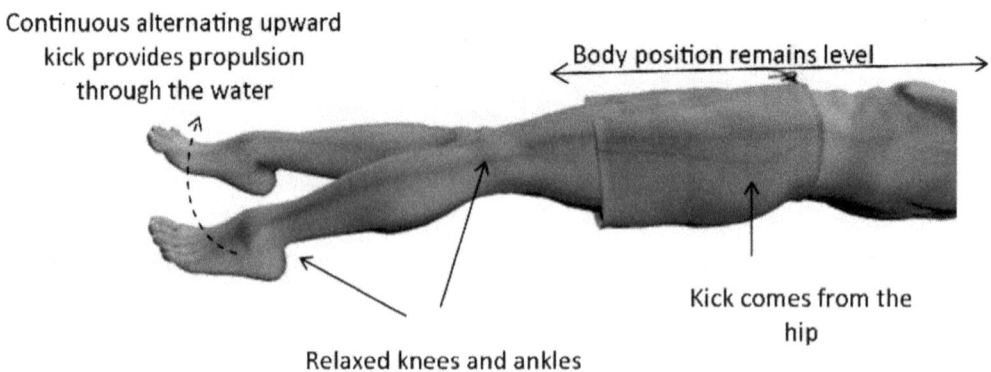

Continuous alternating upward kick provides propulsion through the water

Body position remains level

Kick comes from the hip

Relaxed knees and ankles

The knee should bend slightly and then straighten as the leg kicks upwards. Toes should kick to create a small splash but not break the water surface.

During specific leg practices, the legs kick in a vertical plane. However, the arm action causes the body to roll, making the legs kick part sideways, part vertical and partly to the other side.

Common leg kick mistakes

The most common fault with the leg kick during backstroke is closely related to the body position when the swimmer allows their legs to sink below the water surface. The toes should break the water surface, and the legs kick from the hip with a slight bend at the knee.

An easy exercise to help maintain leg kick technique at the correct level in the water is to hold a float or kickboard across the chest and perform the leg kick.

The float will provide support so that the swimmer can focus on kicking up towards the water surface while maintaining a level head and hips. Only then will the leg kick be at its most efficient.

This same exercise will help iron out another common mistake: kicking from the knee. An excessive knee bend will cost energy and cause the legs to sink gradually.

Performing backstroke kick whilst holding a float will help the swimmer focus on kicking from the hip and not from the knee.

Arms

There are two possible arm actions for backstroke. The bent arm pull is more effective because it is faster and has greater propulsion, and the straight arm pull is used in a more recreational backstroke.

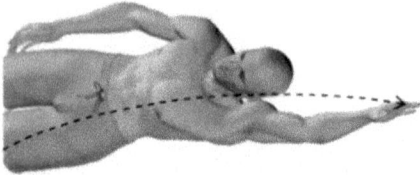

Arm rises upwards, little finger leading and arm brushing the ear

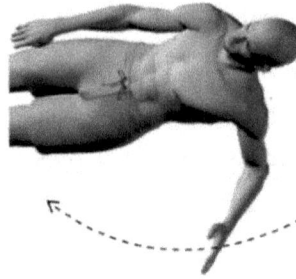

Hand pulls through the water towards the hip

Straight Arm Pull

Entry
The arm should be straight and as in line with the shoulder as possible. The hand should be turned with the palm facing outwards and the little finger entering the water first.

Propulsive Phase
The arm sweeps through the water in a semi-circle, pulling with force just under the water surface to the thigh.

Recovery
The thumb or the back of the hand should exit the water first. The shoulders roll again with the shoulder of the recovering arm rolling upwards. The arm rotates 180 degrees over the shoulder. During recovery, the palm is turned outwards to ensure that the hand enters the water little finger first.

Bent Arm Pull

As the arm pulls through to completion, the overall path should follow an 'S' shape.

Entry
The entry is the same as the straight arm pull, with the little finger entering first, the palm facing out, and the arm close to the shoulder line.

Downward Sweep
The palm should always face the direction of travel. The shoulders roll, and the elbow bends slightly as the arm sweeps downwards and outwards.

Upwards Sweep
As the hand sweeps inline with the shoulder, the palm changes pitch to sweep upwards and inwards. The elbow should then bend to 90 degrees and point to the pool floor.

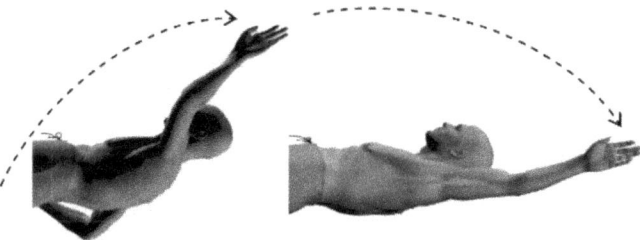

Arm exits the water and brushes past the ear, entering the water little finger first

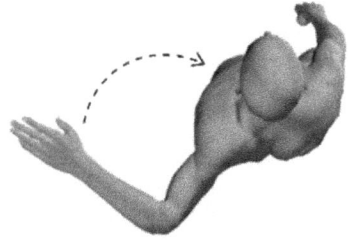

Arm is bent as it pulls through and straightens as it pulls to the thigh

Second Downward Sweep
The arm action then sweeps inwards towards the thigh, and the palm faces downwards. The bent arm action is completed with the arm fully extended and the hand pushing downwards to counterbalance the shoulder roll.

Recovery

The thumb or the back of the hand should exit the water first. The shoulders roll again with the shoulder of the recovering arm rolling upwards. The arm rotates 180 degrees over the shoulder. During recovery, the palm is turned outwards to ensure that the hand enters the water little finger first.

Common arm pull mistakes

Two common faults cause the arm technique for backstroke to become weak and the overall stroke inefficient.

Firstly the upper arm must brush past the ear, and the edge of the hand must enter the water in line with the shoulder. If the hand enters the water wide of the shoulder line, the arm pull will be incomplete and lack power.

Secondly, it is common to perform one arm pull at a time. In other words, one arm completes a whole arm pull cycle before the second arm begins its arm cycle. The arm pulls for backstroke should be continuous where one arm begins to pull as the other arm begins to recover.

Practising the arm technique whilst holding a float on the chest is a good way of ensuring the hand is entering inline with the shoulder and that the arm pull is complete. Once this has been mastered, the swimmer can practice the full stroke to ensure the arms perform continuous cycles.

Breathing

Breathing during backstroke should be relaxed and easy due to the supine body position and face being out of the water throughout the stroke. Most swimmers are neither aware of how they breathe nor the pattern of breathing or point at which a breath is taken.

Breathing should be in time with the recovery of each arm, breathing in with one arm recovery and out with the other. This encourages a breath to be taken at regular intervals.

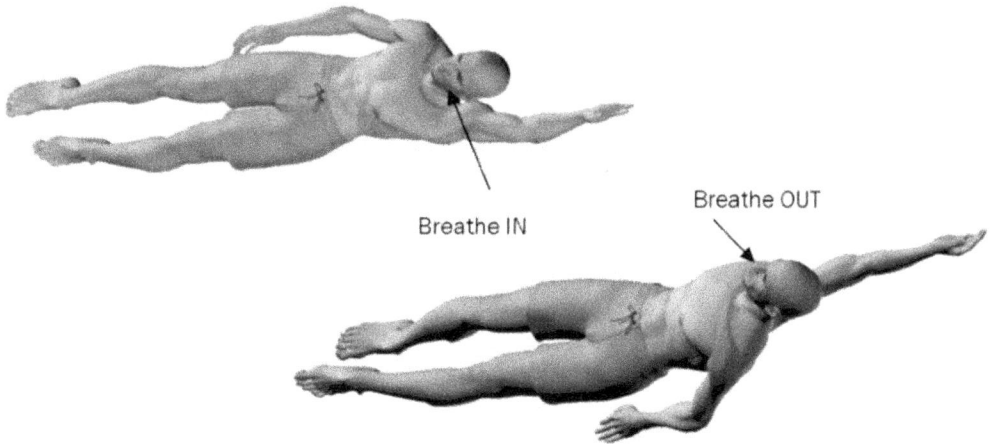

Breathe IN

Breathe OUT

A regular breathing pattern should be encouraged to prevent breath-holding, particularly in beginners.

Common breathing mistakes

Breath-holding is a common mistake made when swimming this stroke, and the result is an exhausted and breathless swimmer. Do you ever feel like you become breathless very quickly when swimming this stroke? Swimming requires fitness and stamina, but this is only one factor.

Breathing technique is essential, and it is common for swimmers, especially beginners, to hold their breath without knowing they are doing so.

Performing the stroke slowly at first or with floats to provide support, swimmers must breathe out and then in again in time with each arm pull. Try to establish a rhythm of breathing through each stroke cycle. This will help prevent breath-holding and unnecessary tiredness and exhaustion.

An established breathing rhythm will help to maintain the timing and coordination of the arms and legs as they pull and kick. It will also assist the swimmer in relaxing and therefore swimming with a calm, controlled and smooth backstroke.

Timing and Coordination

The timing and coordination of the arms and legs develop with practice. Ideally, there should be 6 leg kicks to one arm cycle. The opposite leg kicks downwards at the beginning of each arm pull, which helps balance the body. This may vary according to the swimmer's level of coordination.

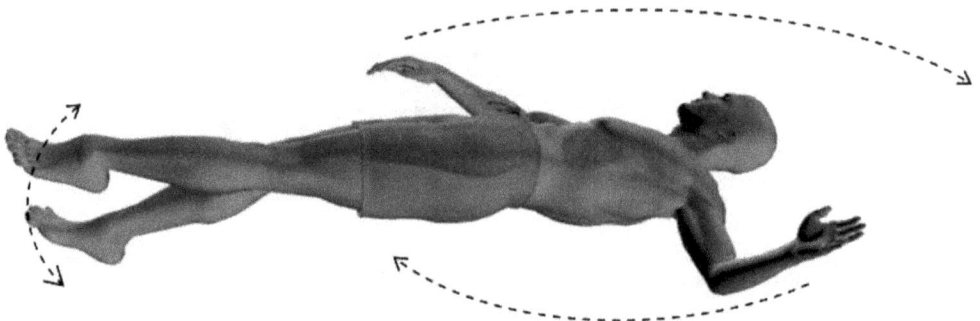

One arm exits the water as the other begins to pull and the leg kick remains continuous

Arm action should be continuous. i.e. when one arm enters and begins to pull, the other should start its recovery phase.

Common timing mistakes

A common mistake is performing one arm cycle at a time, resulting in an uneven and unbalanced stroke overall.

Timing and coordination problems occur with backstroke when the legs are allowed to sink below the water surface. The arms lose their continuity and pull one arm at a time.

Counting in your head can sometimes help to maintain stroke rhythm and timing. If your pupils can perform a 6 beat cycle, they should count to 3 during each arm pull, therefore kicking 3 legs kicks per arm pull.

If a one beat cycle comes more naturally, there should be one leg kick for each arm pull. Performing the stroke slowly at first will help establish the rhythm and timing. Only when pupils are proficient in swimming at a slow, steady pace should you try to increase speed.

With speed increases comes the more significant potential for the timing and coordination to become disrupted and the overall swimming stroke to lose its efficiency.

Backstroke Exercises

**'I hear and I forget
I see and I remember
I do and I understand'**
Confucius

Backstroke Exercises

The lessons plans that follow on from these exercises cover lessons for beginners, intermediate and advanced swimmers. Although these exercises form the foundation from which to teach backstroke, many other exercises are used throughout the lesson plans.

Every swimming teacher has their own 'take' on a particular exercise and many will have more exercises and drills in their repertoire to call upon. Listing all possible backstroke exercises and drills and their variations would be an endless task and therefore beyond the scope of this book.

It is assumed that a swimming teacher will use their professional judgement and experience to make the best use of the exercises and lesson plans outlined here.

Body Position

Floating supine supported by floats

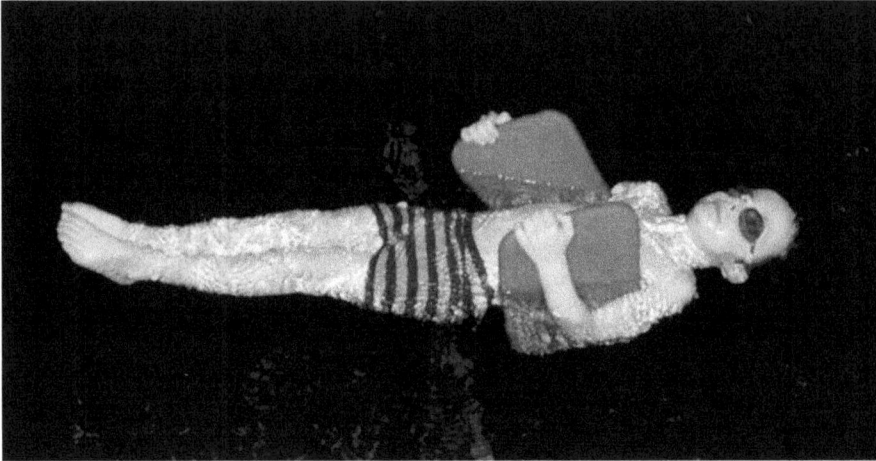

Aim: to gain confidence in a supine position on the water surface.

This exercise is ideal for the nervous swimmer. Support initially can be provided by the teacher or assistant, if he/she is also in the water. 2 floats can then provide support, one placed under each arm, or by a woggle placed under both arms as in the photograph above.

Teaching Points

- Relax
- Make your body flat on top of the water
- Keep your head back
- Push your tummy up to the surface
- Look up to the ceiling
- Keep your head still
- Keep yourself in a long straight line

Teacher's Focus

- Overall body should be horizontal and streamlined
- Head remains still
- Eyes looking upwards and towards the feet
- Hips must be close to the surface
- Legs must be together

Body Position
Floating supine supported by floats

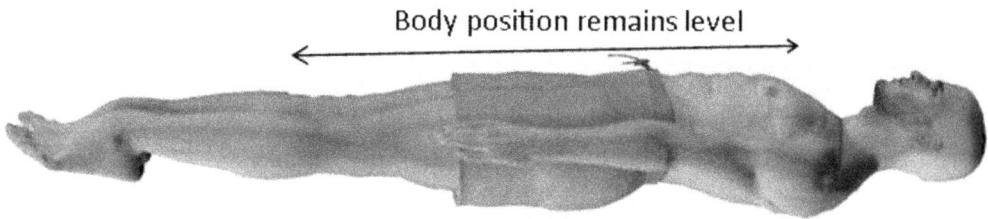

Body position remains level

Common Faults	Remedy
Head raises out of the water	Reiterate the teaching point
Waist and hips sink	Reiterate the teaching point
Failing to maintain a flat position	Assist and encourage relaxation

Body Position

Static supine position, holding a single float

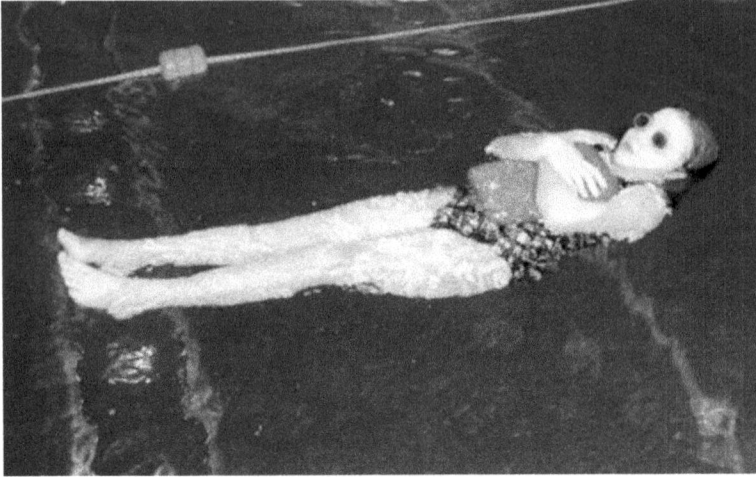

Aim: to develop confidence in a supine position.

Holding a single float across the chest gives security to the nervous swimmer, but is not as stable as a woggle or a float under each arm and so is a subtle and gradual progression. If necessary, this exercise can be performed without a float, as shown in the diagram below, as an additional progression.

Teaching Points
- Relax
- Keep your head back
- Push your tummy up to the surface
- Look up to the ceiling
- Keep your head still

Teacher's Focus
- Overall body should be horizontal
- Head remains still
- Eyes looking upwards
- Hips must be close to the surface
- Legs must be together

Body Position
Static supine position, holding a single float

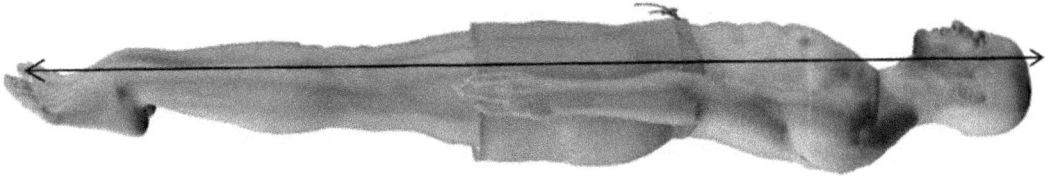

Body position remains horizontal and relaxed

Common Faults	Remedy
Head raises out of the water	Reiterate the teaching point and repeat
Eyes look up but head tips forward	Reiterate the teaching point and repeat
Waist and hips sink	Revert to the previous practice
Head moves about	Reiterate the teaching point
Failing to maintain a straight line	Assist and encourage relaxation

Body Position

Push and glide holding a float

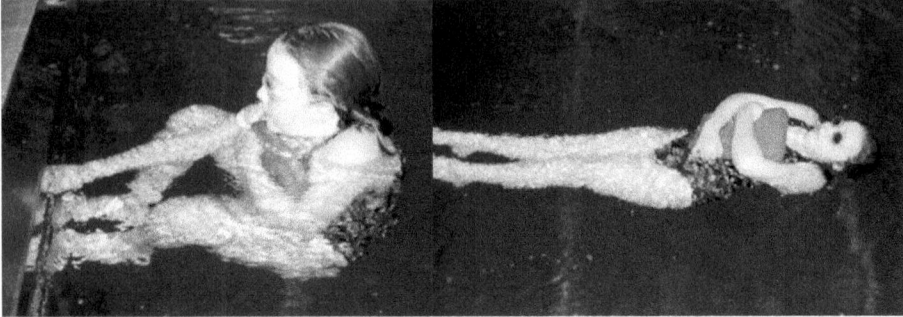

Aim: to gain confidence and move through the water in a supine position.

Holding a float gives added security to the nervous or weak swimmer whilst helping to maintain correct body position.

Teaching Points
- Relax
- Keep your head back and chin up
- Push your tummy up to the surface
- Look up to the ceiling
- Keep your head still
- Push off like a rocket

Teacher's Focus
- Overall body should be horizontal and streamlined
- Head remains still
- Eyes looking upwards
- Hips must be close to the surface
- Legs must be together

Body Position
Push and glide holding a float

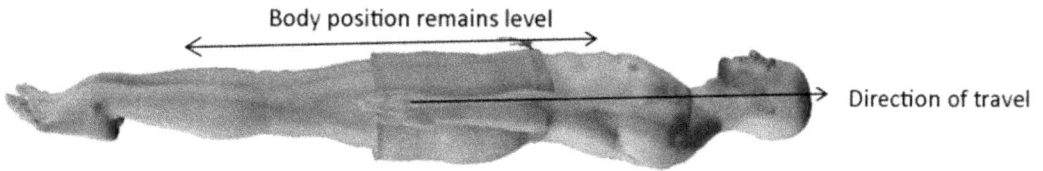

Body position remains level

Direction of travel

Float can be placed on the chest or behind the head as in the photos above.

Common Faults	Remedy
Push off is not hard enough	Reiterate the teaching point and repeat
Head raises out of the wate	Repeat the previous body position practice
Waist and hips sink	Reiterate the teaching point and repeat
Head moves about	Reiterate the teaching point
Failing to maintain a straight line	Assist and encourage relaxation

Body Position

Push and glide from the poolside without floats

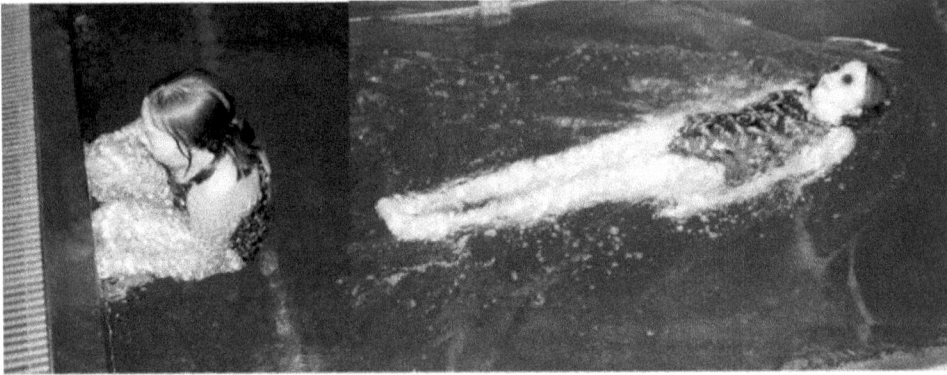

Aim: to encourage correct body position whilst moving.

The swimmer uses the momentum of a push from the poolside. Arms are held by the sides or held straight over the head in more advanced cases.

Teaching Points

- Relax
- Make your body as long as you can
- Push off like a rocket
- Push your tummy up to the surface
- Look up to the ceiling
- Glide in a long straight line

Teacher's Focus

- Overall body should be horizontal and streamlined
- Head remains still
- Eyes looking upwards and towards the feet
- Hips must be close to the surface
- Legs must be together
- Arms are held by the sides

Direction of travel

Water flow

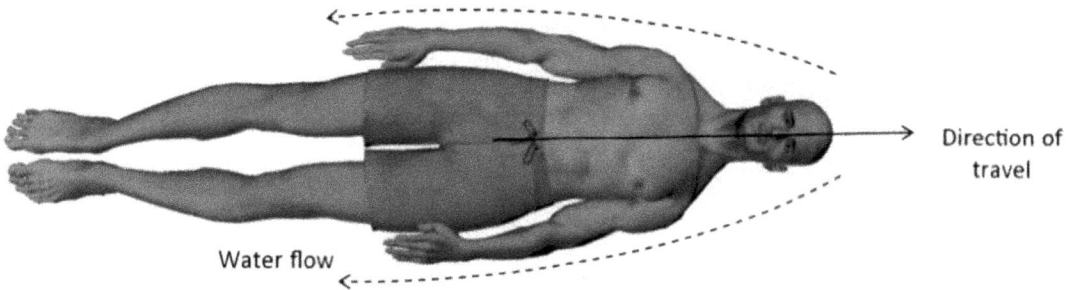

Common Faults	Remedy
Push off is not hard enough	Reiterate the teaching point and repeat
Head raises out of the water	Repeat the previous body position practice
Waist and hips sink	Reiterate the teaching point and repeat
Head moves about	Reiterate the teaching point
Failing to maintain a straight line	Reiterate the teaching point and repeat

Legs

Static practice, sitting on the poolside

Aim: to develop an alternating leg kick action.

The swimmer is positioned sitting on the poolside with feet in the water. Ideal for the nervous beginner to get accustomed to the 'feel' of the water.

Teaching Points

- Point your toes like a ballerina
- Kick from your hips
- Kick with floppy feet
- Keep your legs together
- Make your legs as long as possible

Teacher's Focus

- Kick comes from the hips
- Toes are pointed
- Legs are together
- Slight knee bend
- Ankles are relaxed

Upward kick is continuous and alternating

Ankles are relaxed and toes pointed

Kick comes from the hip

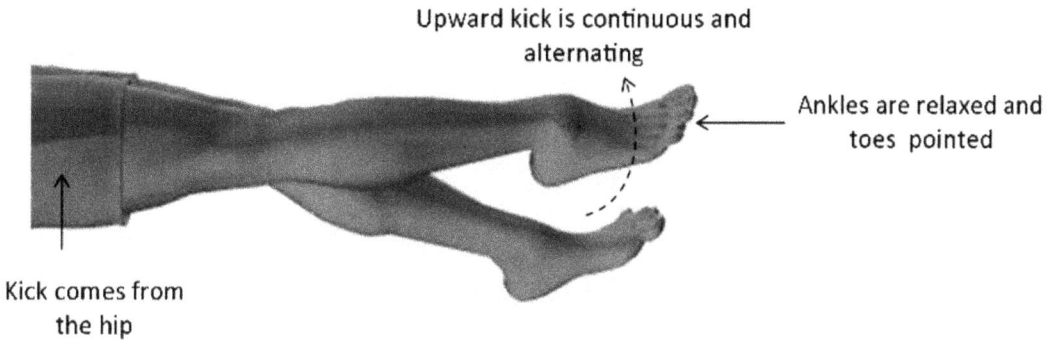

Common Faults	Remedy
Kick comes from the knee	Reiterate teaching point and repeat
Legs kick apart	Check body position and repeat
Toes are turned up	Reiterate the teaching point, demonstrate and repeat
Legs are too 'stiff', not relaxed	Encourage to relax and repeat

Legs

Woggle held under the arms

Aim: to practise and develop correct leg kick action.

This exercise is ideal for the nervous beginner as an introduction to swimming on the back. The stability of the woggle encourages kicking and motion backwards with ease.

Teaching Points

- Point your toes like a ballerina
- Kick from your hips
- Kick with floppy feet
- Make a small splash with your toes

Teacher's Focus

- Kick comes from the hips
- Kick is alternating and continuous
- Kick breaks the water surface
- Hips and tummy up near the surface
- Toes are pointed and ankles relaxed
- Legs are together
- Slight knee bend

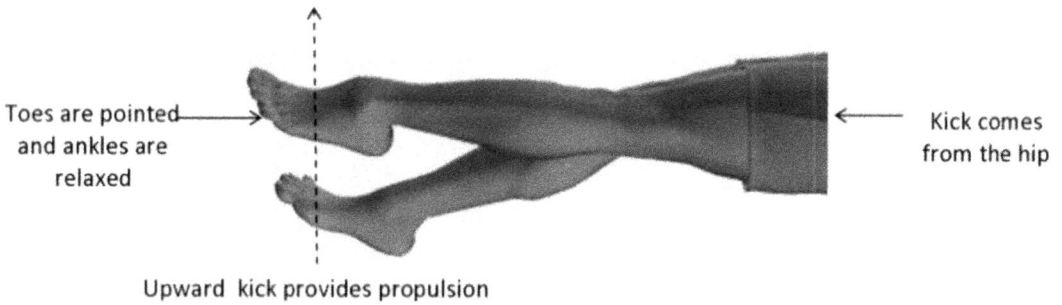

Toes are pointed and ankles are relaxed

Kick comes from the hip

Upward kick provides propulsion

Common Faults	Remedy
Kick comes from the knee	Reiterate teaching point and repeat
Hips sink and legs kick too deep	Check body position and repeat
Toes are turned up	Reiterate the teaching point, demonstrate and repeat
Stiff ankles	Repeat previous leg practice
Legs are too 'stiff', not relaxed	Encourage to relax and repeat

Legs

Float held under each arm

Aim: to practise and develop leg action whilst maintaining correct body position.

Two floats provide good support and encourage a relaxed body position, without creating excessive resistance through the water.

Teaching Points

- Relax and kick hard
- Point your toes like a ballerina
- Kick from your hips
- Kick with floppy feet
- Make a small splash with your toes
- Keep your legs together

Teacher's Focus

- Kick breaks the water surface
- Hips and tummy are up near the surface
- Toes are pointed and ankles relaxed
- Legs are together
- Slight knee bend
- Ankles are relaxed

Body alignment and direction of travel

Continuous alternating upward kick provides propulsion through the water

Common Faults	Remedy
Toes are turned up, causing a lack of motion	Reiterate teaching point and repeat
Head comes up, causing legs to sink	Repeat the earlier body position practices
Hips sink and legs kick too deep	Check the body position and repeat
Legs kick apart	Reiterate the teaching point and repeat

Legs

Float held on the chest

Aim: to allow the correct body position to be maintained whilst the legs kick.

This is a progression from having a float held under each arm. The swimmer is less stable but still has the security of one float held on the chest.

Teaching Points

- Point your toes like a ballerina
- Kick from your hips
- Kick with floppy feet
- Make a small splash with your toes
- Keep your legs together

Teacher's Focus

- Kick comes from the hips
- Kick is alternating and continuous
- Kick breaks the water surface
- Hips and tummy up near the surface
- Legs are together
- Ankles are relaxed and toes pointed

Body position remains level

Ankles are relaxed and toes pointed to provide power to the upward kick

Kick comes from the hip

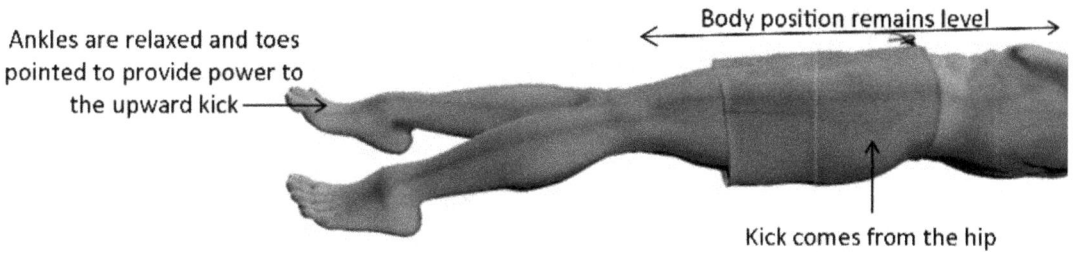

Common Faults	Remedy
Kick comes from the knee	Reiterate teaching point and repeat
Legs are kicking too deep	Repeat the previous leg practice
Toes are turned up	Repeat the earlier poolside practice
Stiff ankles	Reiterate the teaching point and repeat
Legs are too 'stiff', not relaxed	Encourage the pupil to relax and repeat

Legs

Float held behind the head

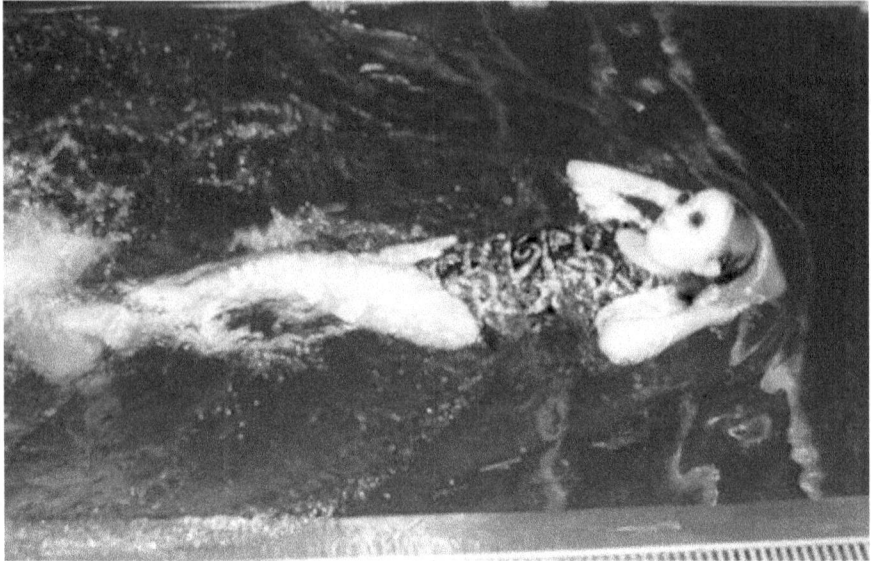

Aim: to encourage correct body position as the legs kick.

The float behind the head helps to keep the chest and hips high. A variation of the exercise with the float held on the chest, this exercise helps to develop leg strength and stamina.

Teaching Points

- Kick from your hips
- Kick with floppy feet
- Make a small splash with your toes
- Keep your legs together

Teacher's Focus

- Kick comes from the hips
- Kick breaks the water surface
- Hips and tummy up near the surface
- Toes are pointed and ankles relaxed
- Legs are together

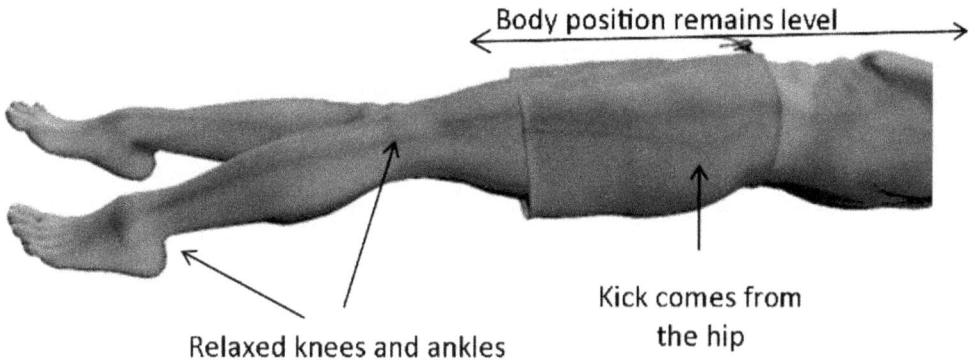

Body position remains level

Kick comes from the hip

Relaxed knees and ankles

Common Faults	Remedy
Kick comes from the knee	Repeat the earlier leg practices
Legs are kicking too deep	Check the body position and repeat
Toes are turned up	Reiterate the teaching point and repeat
Stiff ankles	Reiterate the teaching point and repeat
Legs are too 'stiff', not relaxed	Encourage the pupil to relax and repeat

Legs

Float held over the knees

Aim: to prevent excessive knee bend by holding a float over the knees.

This kicking practice should be performed with the float held on the water surface without the knees hitting it as they kick.

Teaching Points

- Kick with straight legs
- Point your toes like a ballerina
- Stop your knees hitting the float
- Kick with floppy feet

Teacher's Focus

- Kick comes from the hips
- Legs kick without touching the float
- Kick breaks the water surface
- Hips and tummy up near the surface
- Toes are pointed and ankles relaxed

Toes are pointed to provide
power to the upward kick →

Knee is relaxed and
slightly bent

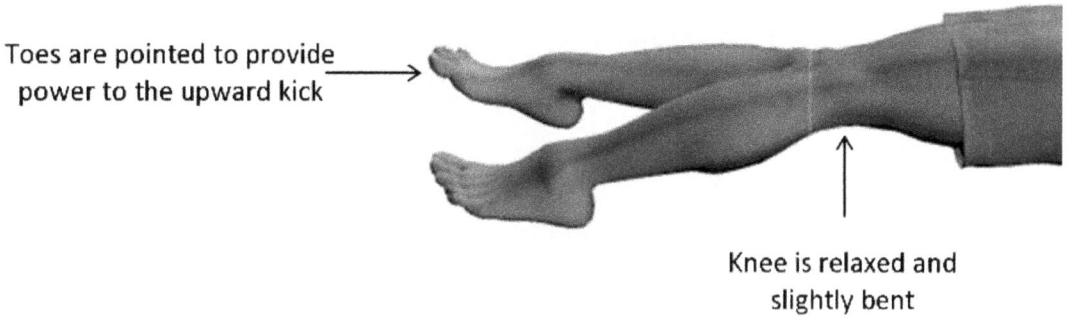

Common Faults	Remedy
Kick comes from the knee	Reiterate the teaching point and repeat
Knees bend and hit the float	Encourage a kick from the hip
Leg kick is too deep	Check the body position and repeat
Float is held up above the water surface	Demonstrate and repeat

Legs

Float held overhead with arms straight

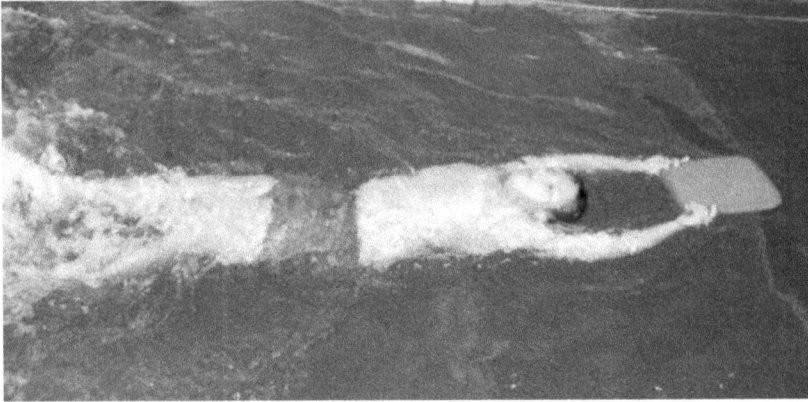

Aim: to enhance a correct body position whilst kicking.

This exercise is a progression from previous leg kick exercises and helps to develop a stronger leg kick.

Teaching Points

- Push your hips and chest up to the surface
- Point your toes like a ballerina
- Make your whole body long and straight
- Kick from your hips
- Stretch out and kick hard

Teacher's Focus

- Kick comes from the hips
- Arms remain either side of the head
- Kick breaks the water surface
- Hips and tummy up near the surface

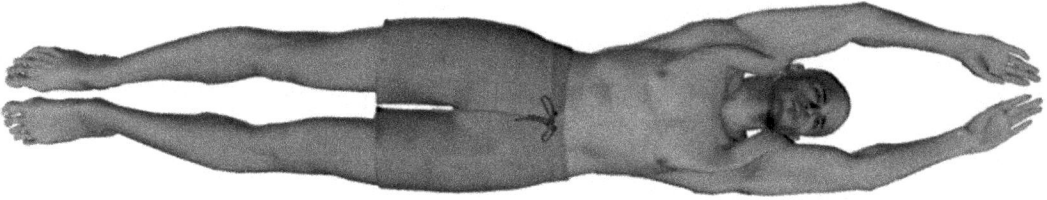

Legs kick and correct body position is maintained throughout.
Note: advanced alternative is shown without holding a float.

Common Faults	Remedy
Head is raised causing hips and legs to sink	Check the body position and repeat
Hips sink and legs kick too deep	Repeat the earlier body position practices
Toes are turned up	Repeat the earlier body position practices
Head is too far back and the upper body sinks	Repeat earlier body position practices

Legs

Kicking with arms by the sides, hands sculling

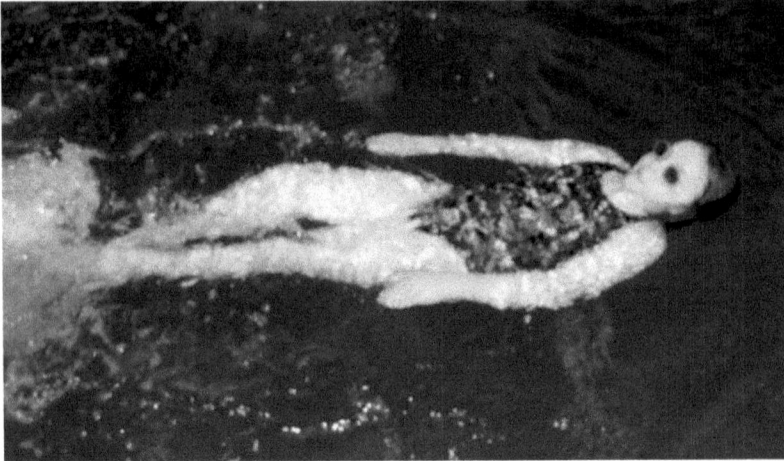

Aim: to practise kicking and maintaining correct body position on the back.

The sculling hand action provides balance and enhances confidence.

Teaching Points

- Relax
- Push your hips and chest up to the surface
- Point your toes like a ballerina
- Kick with floppy feet
- Look up to the sky

Teacher's Focus

- Kick comes from the hips
- Kick is alternating and continuous
- Kick breaks the water surface
- Hips and tummy up near the surface
- Ankles are relaxed and toes are pointed

Body position remains level

Legs kick as previous exercises

Hands sculling by
the sides

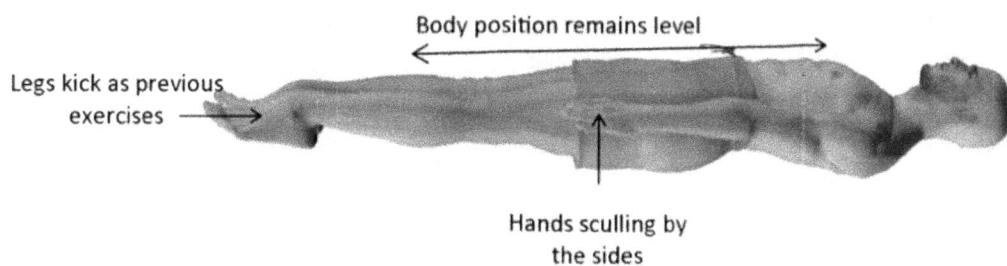

Common Faults	Remedy
Kick comes from the knee	Repeat the earlier leg practices
Hips sink and legs kick too deep	Repeat the earlier body position practices
Head is too far back	Repeat the earlier body position practices
Body is not relaxed	Repeat earlier practices

Arms

Static practice standing on the poolside

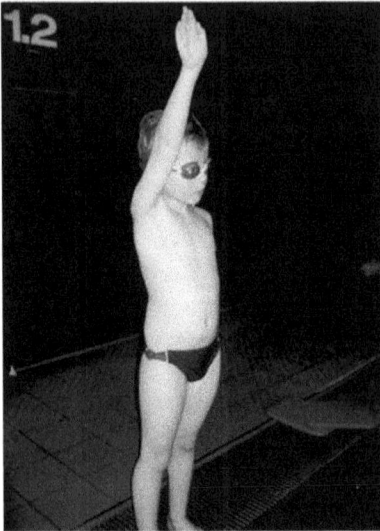

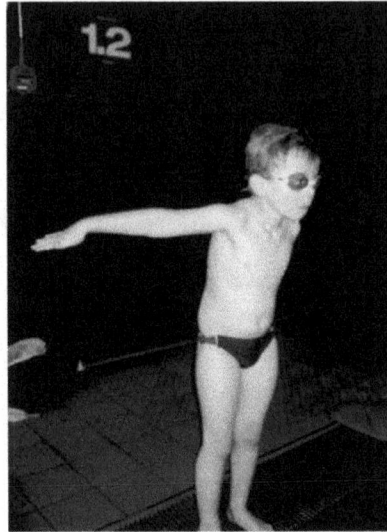

Aim: to practise the arm action in its most basic form.

Standing on the poolside allows the swimmer to develop basic technique in a static position.

Teaching Points

- Arms brush past your ear
- Fingers closed together
- Arms are continuous
- Stretch your arm all the way up to your ear
- Pull down to your side

Teacher's Focus

- Arm action is continuous
- Arms stretch all the way up and brush past the ear
- Arms pull down to the side, towards the hip

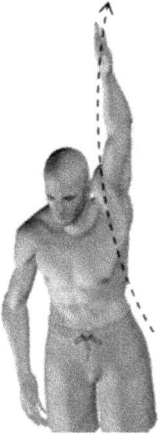

Arm rises upwards, little finger leading and arm brushing the ear

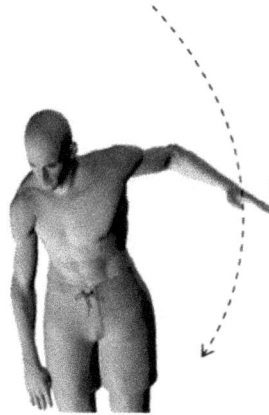

Hand pulls downwards toward the hip

Common Faults	Remedy
Arms are not raising to touch the ear	Demonstrate and repeat
Arms are not pulling down to the side	Demonstrate and repeat
Pausing in-between arm pulls	Reiterate the teaching point and repeat
Arms are bending over the head	Demonstrate and repeat

Arms

Single arm pull with a float held on the chest

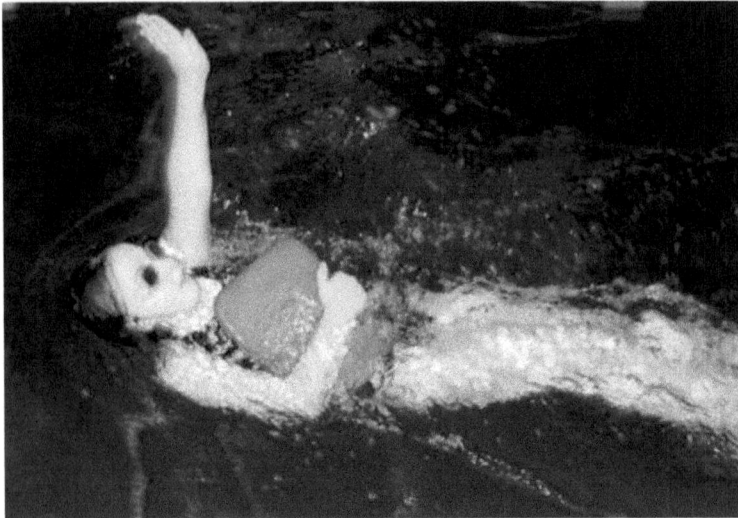

Aim: to develop correct arm action whilst kicking.

The float held on the chest provides support for the beginner and the single arm action allows easy learning without compromising the swimmer's coordination.

Teaching Points

- Arm brushes past your ear
- Pull down to your thigh
- Fingers closed together
- Little finger enters the water first

Teacher's Focus

- Arm action is continuous
- Arms stretch all the way up and brush past the ear
- Arms pull down to the thigh
- Fingers are together
- Little finger enters water first

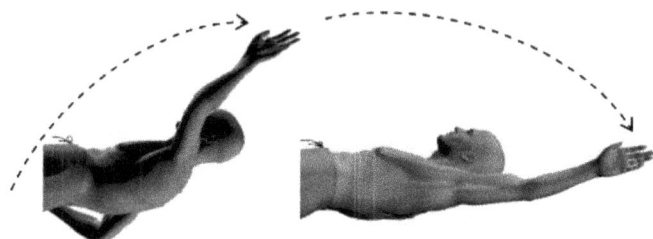

Arm exits the water and brushes past the ear, entering the water little finger first

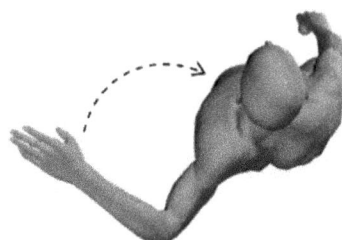

Arm is bent as it pulls through and straightens as it pulls to the thigh

Common Faults	Remedy
Arms are pulling out wide, not brushing the ear	Reiterate the teaching point and repeat
Arms are not pulling down to the side	Reiterate the teaching point and repeat
Arms pull too deep under the water	Repeat the previous arm practice
Fingers are apart	Reiterate teaching point and repeat
Thumb enters the water first	Repeat previous arm practice

Arms

Single arm pull using the lane rope

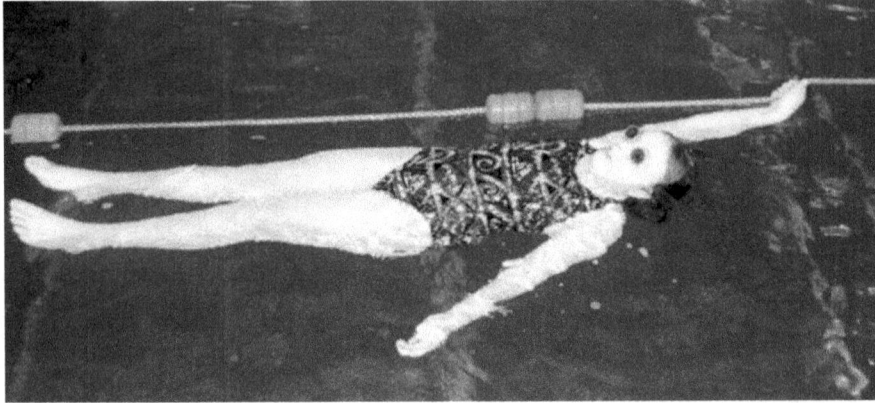

Aim: to develop a bent arm pull using the lane rope to move though the water.

The hand remains fixed on the lane rope as the body is pulled along in the line of the rope. This simulates the bent arm pull action.

Teaching Points

- Use the rope to pull you along
- Arms brush past your ear
- Stretch over and hold the rope behind
- Pull fast down the rope
- Thumb comes out first
- Little finger enters the water first

Teacher's Focus

- Arm action is continuous
- Arms stretch all the way up and brush past the ear
- Arms pull down to the thigh
- Arm action is continuous
- Thumb comes out first

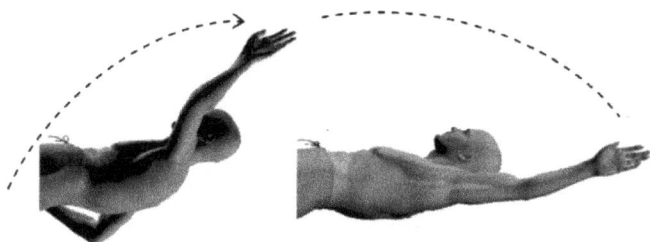

Arm exits the water and brushes past the ear, entering the water little finger first, taking hold of the lane rope

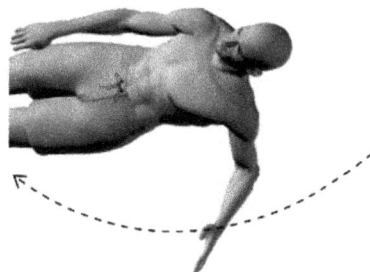

Swimmer pulls from above the head and then pushes past the hip to simulate the bent arm pull action

Common Faults	Remedy
Arms are not pulling down to the side	Reiterate the teaching point and repeat
Elbow is not bending enough	Reiterate the teaching point and repeat
Arms are bending over the head	Repeat the earlier arm practices
Thumb enters the water first	Repeat the earlier arm practices

Arms

Single arm pull with the opposite arm held by the side

Aim: to practise correct arm action without the aid of floats.

This single arm exercise allows focus on one arm whilst the arm held by the side encourages correct body position.

Teaching Points

- Arms brush past your ear
- Arms are continuous
- Pull down to your side
- Pull fast through the water
- Little finger enters the water first

Teacher's Focus

- Arm action is continuous
- Arms stretch all the way up and brush past the ear
- Arms pull down to the thigh
- Shoulders rock with each arm pull
- Little finger enters the water first

Single arm pull with the opposite arm held by the side

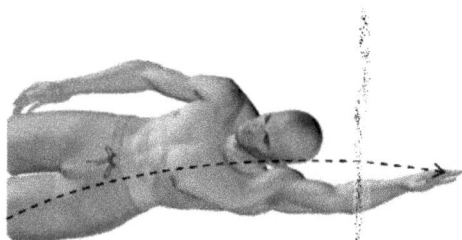

Arm rises upwards, little finger leading and arm brushing the ear

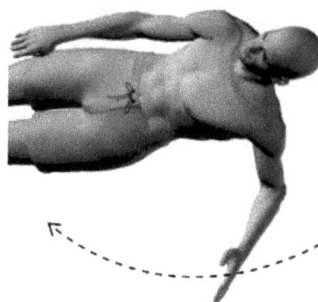

Hand pulls through the water towards the hip

Common Faults	Remedy
Arms are pulling too wide, not brushing the ear	Repeat the earlier arm practices
Arms are not pulling down to the side	Reiterate the teaching point and repeat
Arms pull too deep under the water	Repeat the earlier arm practices
Arms are bending over the head	Repeat the earlier arm practices

Arms

Arms only with pull-buoy held between legs

Aim: to develop a continual arm action using both arms.

The pull-buoy provides support and helps to isolate the arms by preventing the leg kick action. Note: it is normal for the legs to 'sway' from side to side during this exercise.

Teaching Points

- Arms brush past your ear
- Fingers closed together
- Continuous arm action
- Pull hard through the water and down to your side
- Allow your legs to 'sway' side to side

Teacher's Focus

- Arm action is continuous and steady
- Arms stretch all the way over and brush past the ear
- Arms pull down to the thigh
- Shoulders rock evenly side to side

Arms only with pull-buoy held between legs

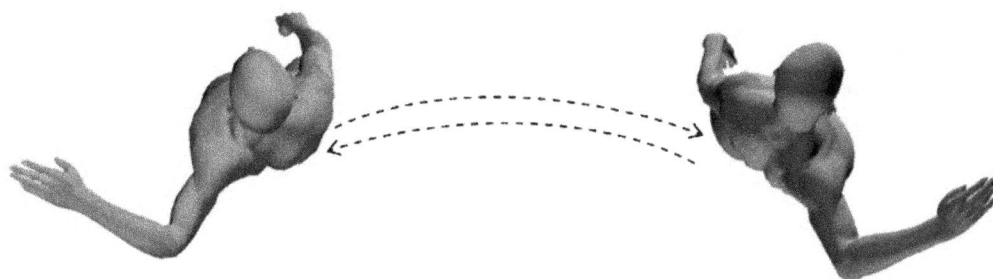

Continual arm action causes an even rocking of the shoulders

Common Faults	Remedy
Pause between arm pulls	Repeat the poolside standing practice
Arms are pulling too wide, not brushing the ear	Reiterate the teaching point and repeat
Arms are not pulling down to the side	Repeat the earlier arm practices
Arms pull too deep under the water	Repeat the earlier arm practices

Breathing

Full stroke with breathing

Aim: to focus on breathing in time with the stroke actions.

The swimmer should breathe in and out in regular rhythm with the arm action. This exercise can be incorporated into any of the previous arm action exercises, depending on the ability of the swimmer.

Teaching Points

- Breathe in time with your arms
- Breathe in with one arm pull and out with the other

Teacher's Focus

- Breathing should be regular and rhythmical

Breathe IN

Breathe OUT

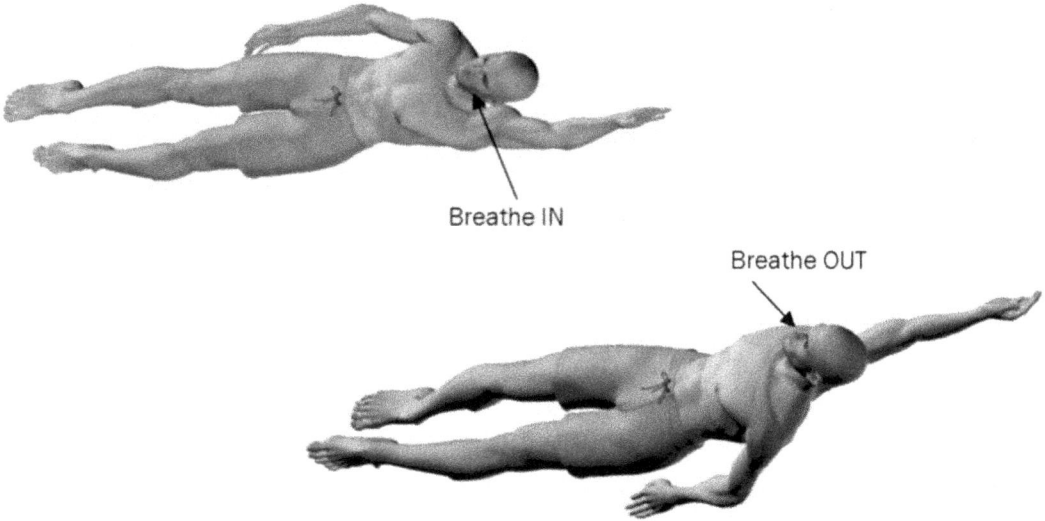

Common Faults	Remedy
Holding the breath	Repeat the static breathing practices
Breathing too rapidly	Reiterate the teaching point and repeat

Timing

Push and glide adding arms and legs

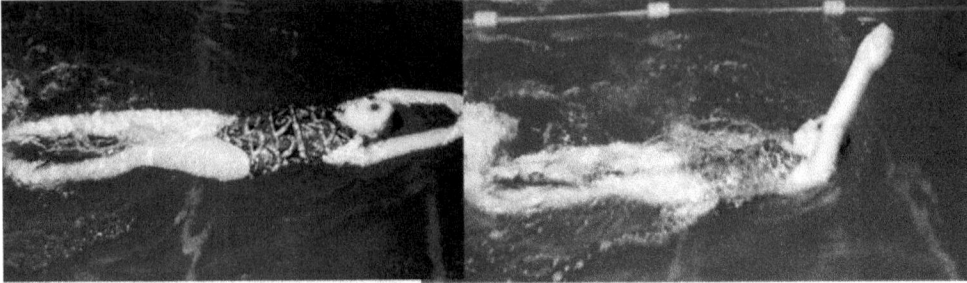

Aim: to practise and develop coordination and stroke timing.

The swimmer performs a push and glide to establish correct body position, then adds arm and leg actions.

Teaching Points

- Count in your head to 3 with each arm pull
- Kick 3 times with each arm pull
- Keep the arm pull continuous
- Keep the leg kick continuous

Teacher's Focus

- 3 leg kicks per arm pull
- Leg kick should be continuous
- Arm action should be regular

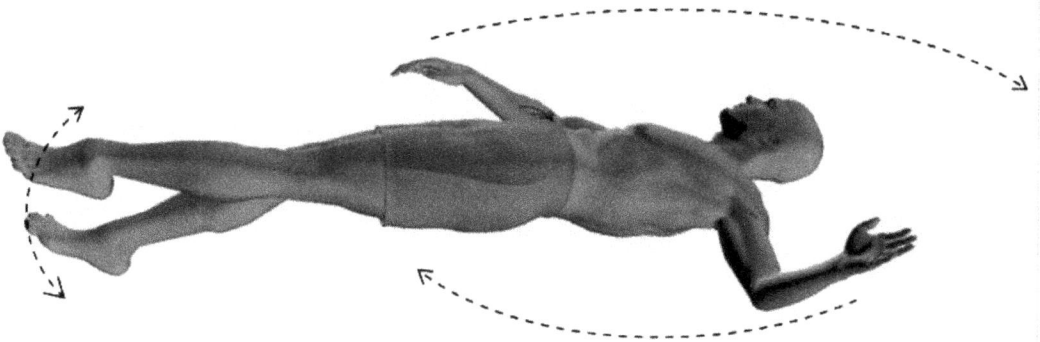

One arm exits the water as the other begins to pull and the leg kick remains continuous

Common Faults	Remedy
One leg kick per arm pull ('one beat cycle')	Reiterate the teaching point and repeat
Continuous leg kick but not enough arm pull	Repeat the earlier arm practices
Arm pull is too irregular	Repeat the earlier arm practices
Stroke cycle is not regular and continuous	Reiterate the teaching point and repeat

Full stroke

Aim: to demonstrate full stroke backstroke showing continuous and alternating arm and leg actions, with correct timing, resulting in a smooth and efficient stroke.

Teaching Points

- Kick from your hips
- Relax
- Keep your hips and tummy at the surface
- Make a small splash with your toes
- Continuous arm action
- Arms brush past your ear and pull to your side

Teacher's Focus

- Body position should be horizontal and flat
- Leg kick should be continuous and alternating
- Arm action is continuous
- Leg kick breaks the water surface
- 3 legs kicks per arm pull

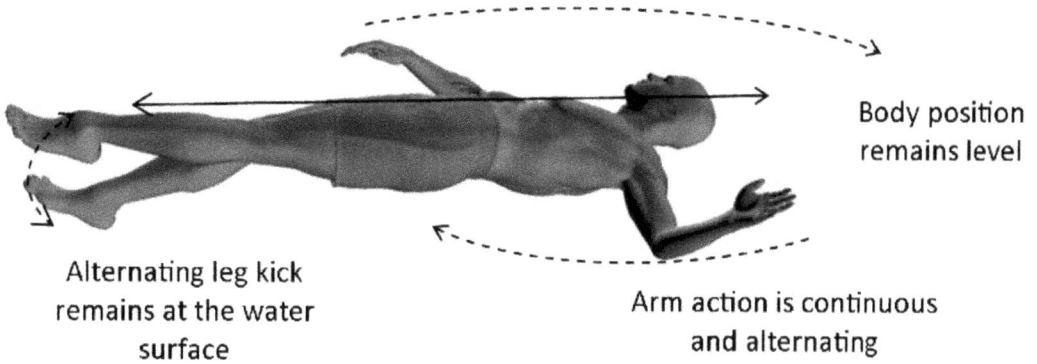

Body position remains level

Alternating leg kick remains at the water surface

Arm action is continuous and alternating

Common Faults	Remedy
Hips and abdomen sink	Repeat the earlier body position practice
Legs kick too deep or weak	Repeat the earlier leg practices
Arms pull one at a time	Repeat the earlier arm practices
Arms pull too wide or too deep	Reiterate the teaching point and repeat

Lesson Plans

Lesson Plan Layout

Lesson Plan #2

Lesson type: full stroke front crawl

Level: adult or child intermediate

Previous learning: basic front crawl technique

Lesson aim: to progress and develop the whole stroke

Equipment: floats, pull buoys, sinkers and hoop

Lesson type: the part of backstroke that this lesson focuses on. For example, **Backstroke Leg Kick**.

Level: who the lesson is aimed at if they are beginners, intermediate or advanced level. For example, **Child Beginner.**

Previous learning: the aspects of swimming the pupil is expected to have covered before this lesson. For example, **basic front paddle**. The pupil is *not* expected to have completely mastered an aspect of swimming but should have had some experience of learning it.

Lesson aim: the lesson objective or desired outcome of the lesson. For example, **'to learn basic backstroke body position and introduce the leg kick'**.

Equipment: the equipment you will need for this lesson. For example, **'floats, buoyancy aids and hoop'**.

Lesson Sequences

Lesson plans are laid out in a sequence (beginner, intermediate, advanced) to give the teacher easy reference to other lessons, exercises and activities in the sequence. This should allow for easier differentiation across varying abilities.

Lesson plans do not have to be followed in sequence, although they can be if you wish. Each plan has its own aim and therefore can be used in sequence with other lessons aimed at that level, to suit the individual pupil or pupils.

These lesson plans and the exercises and activities in them are set out as a guide. Every pupil is different and will interpret and respond to exercises and teaching points in their own way, therefore as a swimming teacher it is important to be flexible in your approach. In other words, where a pupil is finding a particular exercise difficult, chose an easier exercise from a previous plan. Where a pupil is not quite grasping the concept of what you are teaching, try using a different phrase or teaching point.

Teaching Points

Teaching points are our 'magic words'. Having a variety of them in our virtual tool kit can be extremely useful. For example, when you say to a pupil 'point your toes and they just don't get it, you change the teaching point to 'kick with floppy feet'. All of sudden they are kicking with relaxed ankles and pointed toes.

Learning to be creative with our teaching points can be a very powerful skill and can be the difference between a pupil struggling and that light bulb moment when they suddenly understand and can do it.

Organising Your Swimmers

The way you chose to organise your swimmers as they swim off to perform a given exercise is vital to maintaining a safe learning environment and to monitor their progress.

The organisation column of the lesson plans make a suggestion but you will have to use your professional judgement, based on the size of your class and swimming lesson area available in your pool.

The suggestions are:

All together - you instruct all swimmers to go at the same time. Ideal if you have sufficient space and can be unsafe if you do not.

Waves - number your swimmers 1 and 2 alternately (or more if you have a large class). Then instruct all numbers 1's to go first, followed by the number 2's and so on if you have more. This is a good way of monitoring swimmers and also a great way to organise large classes of advanced swimmers.

One-by-one - sending each swimmer off one at a time. This is an ideal way to closely monitor each pupil.

Getting The Timing Right

All swimming pools vary in their dimensions and often larger pools have an area roped off for swimming lessons, so the whole pool is rarely used. These plans assume that beginner and intermediate swimmers will swim widths and advanced swimmers will swim lengths. The size of the width and length in *your* pool might not fit with how these plans are formatted and you may wish to use your professional judgment to change them to fit with your circumstances.

The duration of most swimming lessons is about 30 minutes. The timings of each exercise in these lesson plans are a guide and again, your professional judgement can be used to adjust them to suit your pupils and your pool size.

If you begin to discover that you are racing through the lesson and will have time left over, remember any exercise can be repeated. Repeating an exercise will enhance a pupil's strength, stamina and overall ability. A different teaching point can also be used to help those that perhaps did not quite get it the first time around.

Important Terminology:

Prone - 'facing downwards'. For example, a prone push and glide is performed in the face-down position.

Supine - 'facing downwards' For example, a supine star float is performed on the back, facing upwards.

'By failing to prepare
you are preparing to fail.'
Benjamin Franklin

Lesson Plan #1

Lesson type: full stroke backstroke

Level: adult or child beginner
Previous learning: basic alternating kicking and supine floating
Lesson aim: to learn the basics of backstroke and experience the whole stroke
Equipment: floats, woggle, buoyancy aids if needed and hoop

Exercise/Activity	Teaching Points	Organisation	Duration
Entry: swivel or steps entry	enter slowly	all together	1 min
Warm up: 2 widths any stroke with buoyancy aids if needed	take your time	all together	3 mins
Main Theme: kicking supine with a woggle under the arms	relax and kick	all together	2 mins
supine push and glide, holding floats if needed	hips up and stretch	waves	3 mins
supine kicking with a float held on the chest	kick with pointed toes	waves	3 mins
single arm pulls with a float held on the chest	arm stretches up and back	waves	3 mins
single arm pulls using the opposite arm with a float held on the chest	fingers together	waves	3 mins
2 widths full stroke backstroke	kick and pull continuously	waves	3 mins
Contrasting Activity: prone star float	deep breath and relax	2 or 3 at a time	3 mins
sitting dive through a hoop at the surface	head tucked down	2 or 3 at a time	3 mins
Exit: using the pool steps or over the poolside	take your time	one by one	1 min

Total time: 28 minutes

Lesson #1 Assessment

Lesson Objective: to learn each part of basic backstroke and experience the whole stroke.

Below average	Average	Above average
😐	🙂	😎
Attempts to demonstrate but does not show the correct technique	Able to perform most of the technique correctly some of the time	Performs the technique correctly most of the time

Assessment	😐	🙂	😎
Head is facing upwards			
Hips are at or near the surface			
Legs kick alternately			
Toes are pointed			
Arm pulls are continuous			

Lesson Plan #2

Lesson type: full stroke backstroke
Level: adult or child intermediate
Previous learning: basic backstroke technique
Lesson aim: to progress and develop the whole stroke to an intermediate level
Equipment: floats, pull buoy, sinkers and hoop

Exercise/Activity	Teaching Points	Organisation	Duration
Entry: swivel or sitting dive entry	enter slowly	waves	1 min
Warm up: 2 widths any stroke	take your time	all together	3 mins
Main Theme: 2 widths full stroke backstroke with buoyancy aids if needed	pull and kick continuously	waves	2 mins
supine push and glide from the poolside	head back, looking upwards	one by one	3 mins
supine kicking with a float behind the head	kick with floppy feet	waves	3 mins
arm pulls with a pull buoy	pull through to your thighs	waves	3 mins
arm pulls with a pull buoy, adding breathing	pull and blow	waves	3 mins
full stroke backstroke without buoyancy aids	kick your hands forwards	waves	3 mins
Contrasting Activity: head first surface dives, collecting sinkers placed apart	deep breath and dig down	one by one	3 mins
dolphin kick through a hoop at the surface	swim like a mermaid	one by one	3 mins
Exit: using the pool steps or over the poolside	take your time	one by one	1 min

Total time: 28 minutes

Lesson #2 Assessment

Lesson Objective: to progress and develop the whole stroke to an intermediate level.

Below average	Average	Above average
😐	🙂	😎
Attempts to demonstrate but does not show the correct technique	Able to perform most of the technique correctly some of the time	Performs the technique correctly most of the time

Assessment	😐	🙂	😎
Head is facing upwards with ears in the water			
Hips and tummy are at water surface			
Legs kick alternately with relaxed ankles			
Toes are pointed			
Arms pull through to the thighs			

Lesson Plan #3

Lesson type: full stroke backstroke
Level: adult or child advanced
Previous learning: full stroke backstroke
Lesson aim: to develop and fine-tune technique for the whole stroke
Equipment: floats

Exercise/Activity	Teaching Points	Organisation	Duration
Entry: sitting or shallow dive entry	take your time	waves	1 min
Warm up: 2 lengths any stroke	take your time	all together	3 mins
Main Theme: 2 lengths full stroke backstroke	stretch and glide	waves	2 mins
supine push and glide with arms extended	hands together and stretch	waves	3 mins
supine kicking with arms extended	kick from the hips	waves	3 mins
single arm pulls using a lane rope to help simulate bent arm pull technique	pull through your body line	waves	3 mins
full stroke using bent arm pull action	one arm pulls as the other recovers	waves	3 mins
2 lengths full stroke backstroke	continuous flowing strokes	waves	3 mins
Contrasting Activity: dolphin kick underwater, arms by sides	lead with your head	waves	3 mins
treading water	head above the water	waves	3 mins
Exit: using the pool steps or over the poolside	take your time	one by one	1 min

Total time: 28 minutes

Lesson #3 Assessment

Lesson Objective: to develop and fine-tune technique for the whole stroke.		
Below average	**Average**	**Above average**
😐	🙂	😎
Attempts to demonstrate but does not show the correct technique	**Able to perform most of the technique correctly some of the time**	**Performs the technique correctly most of the time**

Assessment	😐	🙂	😎
Body position is flat and streamlined			
Head is back with ears in the water			
Leg kicks are relaxed and from the hips			
Ankles are relaxed with toes pointed			
One arm pulls as the other recovers			
Stroke movements are continuous and flowing			

Lesson Plan #4

Lesson type: backstroke body position

Level: adult or child beginner
Previous learning: basic back paddle and supine floating
Lesson aim: to learn basic backstroke body position
Equipment: floats, buoyancy aids and sinkers as necessary

Exercise/Activity	Teaching Points	Organisation	Duration
Entry: swivel entry	enter slowly	all together	1 min
Warm up: 2 widths any stroke using buoyancy aids	slow and gentle swim	all together	3 mins
Main Theme: static floating with a float under each arm	relax and keep still	all together	2 mins
static floating with one float held on the chest	keeps your hips up	all together	2 mins
supine push and glide, holding a float	push hips to the surface	one by one	3 mins
push and glide with a float, adding leg kicks	relax and stretch	waves	3 mins
push and glide without buoyancy aids	push off like a rocket	waves	3 mins
push and glide adding kicking and any arm action to support (eg sculling)	look upwards and keep your body flat	waves	3 mins
Contrasting Activity: submerging to collect an object	take your time	2 or 3 at a time	3 mins
submerging to collect objects placed apart	deep breath and relax	2 or 3 at a time	3 mins
Exit: using the pool steps or over the poolside	take your time	one by one	1 min

Total time: 27 minutes

Lesson #4 Assessment

Lesson Objective: to learn basic backstroke body position.		
Below average	**Average**	**Above average**
😐	🙂	😎
Attempts to demonstrate but does not show the correct technique	Able to perform most of the technique correctly some of the time	Performs the technique correctly most of the time

Assessment	😐	🙂	😎
Face is looking upwards			
Body position is flat			
Legs and feet are together			
Hands are at the sides			
Hips are level			
Shoulders are level			

Lesson Plan #5

Lesson type: backstroke body position
Level: adult or child intermediate
Previous learning: basic backstroke backstroke technique
Lesson aim: to improve basic backstroke body position and shape
Equipment: floats and/or woggles and hoop

Exercise/Activity	Teaching Points	Organisation	Duration
Entry: swivel entry	enter slowly	all together	1 min
Warm up: 2 widths any stroke without using buoyancy aids	take your time	all together	3 mins
Main Theme: 2 widths full stroke backstroke	continuous arms and legs	waves	3 mins
supine push and glide, with a float if needed	push hips to the surface	waves	3 mins
push and glide without buoyancy aids	push off like a rocket	waves	3 mins
push and glide with arms extended	streamlined shape hands together	waves	3 mins
push and glide with arms extended, adding leg kicks	keep your body flat and stretched	waves	3 mins
2 widths full stroke backstroke	continuous arms and legs	waves	3 mins
Contrasting Activity: forward somersault from a push and glide	tuck chin on chest	2 or 3 at a time	3 mins
sitting dive through a submerged hoop	hands together	2 or 3 at a time	3 mins
Exit: using the pool steps or over the poolside	take your time	one by one	1 min

Total time: 29 minutes

Lesson #5 Assessment

Lesson Objective: to improve basic backstroke body position and shape.		
Below average	**Average**	**Above average**
😐	🙂	😎
Attempts to demonstrate but does not show the correct technique	Able to perform most of the technique correctly some of the time	Performs the technique correctly most of the time

Assessment	😐	🙂	😎
Face is looking upwards with ears in the water			
Body position is flat and streamlined			
Legs and feet are together			
Hands are together when extended above the head			
Hips and shoulders are level			

Lesson Plan #6

Lesson type: backstroke body position
Level: adult or child advanced
Previous learning: full stroke backstroke
Lesson aim: to develop and fine-tune backstroke body position and shape
Equipment: buoyancy aids if needed

Exercise/Activity	Teaching Points	Organisation	Duration
Entry: sitting or shallow dive entry	take your time	all together	1 min
Warm up: 2 lengths any stroke	steady pace	all together	3 mins
Main Theme: 2 lengths full stroke backstroke	let the stroke flow	all together	3 mins
push and glide with arms extended	streamlined shape hands together	waves	3 mins
push and glide with arms extended, adding leg kicks	keep your body flat and stretched	waves	3 mins
push and glide with arms extended, adding arm pulls	stretch arms up to maintain streamlined shape	waves	3 mins
supine push and glide to submerge and kick underwater for distance	streamlined shape underwater	waves	3 mins
2 lengths full stroke backstroke from racing start	flat and level body position	waves	3 mins
Contrasting Activity: prone push and glide and rotate to supine position	keep head level	2 or 3 at a time	3 mins
any stroke with somersault mid swim	head down, chin to chest	2 or 3 at a time	3 mins
Exit: using the pool steps or over the poolside	take your time	all together	1 min

Total time: 29 minutes

Lesson #6 Assessment

Lesson Objective: to develop and fine-tune backstroke body position and shape.		
Below average	**Average**	**Above average**
😐	🙂	😎
Attempts to demonstrate but does not show the correct technique	**Able to perform most of the technique correctly some of the time**	**Performs the technique correctly most of the time**

Assessment	😐	🙂	😎
Face is looking upwards with ears in the water			
Body position is flat and streamlined whilst kicking and pulling			
Legs and feet are together			
Hands are together when extended above the head			
Hips and shoulders are level when gliding			
Head remains in a neutral position whilst gliding			

Lesson Plan #7

Lesson type: backstroke leg kick
Level: adult or child beginner
Previous learning: basic back paddle
Lesson aim: to learn basic backstroke kicking action
Equipment: floats, buoyancy aids, sinkers and hoop

Exercise/Activity	Teaching Points	Organisation	Duration
Entry: swivel entry	enter slowly	all together	1 min
Warm up: 2 widths any stroke using buoyancy aids	slow and gentle swim	all together	3 mins
Main Theme: sitting on poolside, kicking legs	kick from your hips	all together	2 mins
kicking with woggle under arms	kick with floppy feet	waves	3 mins
kicking with a float held behind the head	push hips to the surface	waves	3 mins
kicking with a float held on the chest	kick with straight legs	waves	3 mins
push and glide, adding leg kicks	pointed toes	waves	3 mins
full stroke backstroke	continuous leg kick	waves	3 mins
Contrasting Activity: jump in and swim through a hoop	jump away from the side	one by one	3 mins
submerging to collect an object	deep breath and relax	2 or 3 at a time	3 mins
Exit: using the pool steps or over the poolside	take your time	one by one	1 min

Total time: 28 minutes

Lesson #7 Assessment

Lesson Objective: to learn basic backstroke leg kick and introduce breathing.		
Below average	**Average**	**Above average**
😐	🙂	😎
Attempts to demonstrate but does not show the correct technique	Able to perform most of the technique correctly some of the time	Performs the technique correctly most of the time

Assessment	😐	🙂	😎
Legs kicks are alternating			
Legs are straight and together			
Kick comes from the hips			
Toes are pointed			

Lesson Plan #8

Lesson type: backstroke leg kick
Level: adult or child intermediate
Previous learning: basic backstroke technique
Lesson aim: to strengthen and develop basic backstroke leg kick
Equipment: floats, buoyancy aids and hoop

Exercise/Activity	Teaching Points	Organisation	Duration
Entry: swivel or sitting dive entry	enter slowly	all together	1 min
Warm up: 2 widths any stroke	take your time	all together	3 mins
Main Theme: kicking with a float held under each arm	toes pointed	all together	2 mins
kicking with a float held behind the head	kick from the hips	waves	3 mins
kicking with one float held on the chest	kick with floppy feet	waves	3 mins
kicking with one float held, arms extended	kick with long legs	waves	3 mins
push and glide adding leg kicks	toes make a small splash	waves	3 mins
2 widths full stroke backstroke	relaxed, flowing kicks	waves	3 mins
Contrasting Activity: sitting dives	chin to chest	one by one	3 mins
push and glide through a submerged hoop	hands and feet together	one by one	3 mins
Exit: using the pool steps	take your time	one by one	1 min

Total time: 28 minutes

Lesson #8 Assessment

Lesson Objective: to strengthen and develop basic backstroke leg kick.		
Below average	**Average**	**Above average**
🙂	🙂	😎
Attempts to demonstrate but does not show the correct technique	Able to perform most of the technique correctly some of the time	Performs the technique correctly most of the time

Assessment	😐	🙂	😎
Legs kicks are continuous and alternating			
Legs are straight and together			
Kick comes from the hips			
Toes are pointed and ankles relaxed			

Lesson Plan #9

Lesson type: backstroke leg kick
Level: adult or child advanced
Previous learning: full stroke backstroke
Lesson aim: to develop and perfect backstroke leg kick
Equipment: floats or kickboards, fins

Exercise/Activity	Teaching Points	Organisation	Duration
Entry: sitting or shallow dive entry	take your time	waves	1 min
Warm up: 2 lengths any stroke	take your time	all together	3 mins
Main Theme: 2 lengths full stroke backstroke	smooth flowing movements	waves	3 mins
kicking with a float held behind the head (position the float to increase resistance)	kick from the hips	waves	3 mins
kicking with one float held, arms extended	kick with long legs	waves	3 mins
push and glide with arms extended, adding leg kicks	toes make a small splash	waves	3 mins
Repeat any of the above drills using fins	relaxed, flowing kicks	waves	3 mins
2 lengths full stroke backstroke	smooth flowing movements	waves	3 mins
Contrasting Activity: push and glide into forward somersault	arms pull down to rotate	2 or 3 at a time	2 mins
supine push and glide into somersault	tuck chin to chest	2 or 3 at a time	2 mins
Exit: using the pool steps	take your time	waves	1 min

Total time: 27 minutes

Lesson #9 Assessment

Lesson Objective: to develop and perfect backstroke leg kick.		
Below average	**Average**	**Above average**
😐	🙂	😎
Attempts to demonstrate but does not show the correct technique	Able to perform most of the technique correctly some of the time	Performs the technique correctly most of the time

Assessment	😐	🙂	😎
Legs kicks are continuous and alternating			
Legs are straight and together			
Kick comes from the hips			
Toes are pointed and ankles relaxed			

Lesson Plan #10

Lesson type: backstroke arms
Level: adult or child beginner
Previous learning: basic back paddle
Lesson aim: to learn basic backstroke arm action
Equipment: floats, buoyancy aids and sinkers as necessary

Exercise/Activity	Teaching Points	Organisation	Duration
Entry: swivel entry	enter slowly	all together	1 min
Warm up: 2 widths any stroke using buoyancy aids	slow and gentle swim	all together	3 mins
Main Theme: standing on poolside, practice arm action	stretch up tall	all together	2 mins
single arm pull with float held on the chest	arm brushes your ear	waves	3 mins
repeat above exercise with the opposite arm	pull down to your side	waves	3 mins
single arm pull with one arm held by the side	thumb exists first	waves	3 mins
repeat above exercise with the opposite arm	little finger enters first	waves	3 mins
full stroke backstroke	continuous arm pull	waves	3 mins
Contrasting Activity: prone star float	deep breath and relax	2 or 3 at a time	3 mins
submerging to collect an object	deep breath and reach down	2 or 3 at a time	3 mins
Exit: using the pool steps or over the poolside	take your time	one by one/all together	1 min

Total time: 28 minutes

Lesson #10 Assessment

Lesson Objective: to learn and practice basic backstroke arm pull.		
Below average	**Average**	**Above average**
😐	🙂	😎
Attempts to demonstrate but does not show the correct technique	Able to perform most of the technique correctly some of the time	Performs the technique correctly most of the time

Assessment	😐	🙂	😎
Arm pulls are continuous			
Hand enters the water little finger first			
Fingers are together			
Arms are straight on entry			

Lesson Plan #11

Lesson type: backstroke arms
Level: adult or child intermediate
Previous learning: basic backstroke technique
Lesson aim: to develop and progress backstroke arm technique
Equipment: floats and/or woggles and sinkers

Exercise/Activity	Teaching Points	Organisation	Duration
Entry: swivel entry or sitting dive entry	take your time	all together	1 min
Warm up: 2 widths any stroke	continuous swimming	all together	2 mins
Main Theme: 2 widths full stroke backstroke	relaxed, smooth movements	all together	3 mins
arm action with a float held on the chest. Opposite arm on return width	fingers together	waves	3 mins
single arm pull with one arm held by the side	thumb exists first	waves	3 mins
repeat above exercise with the opposite arm	little finger enters first	waves	3 mins
alternating arm pulls with a pull buoy held between the legs	one arm pulls and the other recovers	all together	3 mins
full stroke backstroke	smooth flowing movements	all together	3 mins
Contrasting Activity: treading water	mouth and nose out of the water	one by one	2 mins
retrieve an object from the pool floor and return it to the poolside	eyes open	one by one	4 mins
Exit: using the pool steps or over the poolside	take your time	one by one	1 min

Total time: 28 minutes

Lesson #11 Assessment

Lesson Objective: to progress basic backstroke arm action and introduce breathing.		
Below average	**Average**	**Above average**
😐	🙂	😎
Attempts to demonstrate but does not show the correct technique	Able to perform most of the technique correctly some of the time	Performs the technique correctly most of the time

Assessment	😐	🙂	😎
Arm pulls are continuous and alternating			
Hand enters the water little finger first			
Fingers are together			
Arms are straight on entry			
Hand enters the water inline with the shoulder			

Lesson Plan #12

Lesson type: backstroke arms
Level: adult or child advanced
Previous learning: full stroke backstroke
Lesson aim: to develop and fine-tune backstroke arm action
Equipment: hand paddles

Exercise/Activity	Teaching Points	Organisation	Duration
Entry: sitting or shallow dive entry	take your time	waves	1 min
Warm up: 2 lengths any stroke	take your time	all together	3 mins
Main Theme: 2 lengths full stroke backstroke	let your movements flow	waves	3 mins
single arm pull with one arm held by the side (opposite arm on return)	thumb exists first	waves	3 mins
alternating arm pulls with a pull buoy held between the legs	one arm pulls and the other recovers	waves	3 mins
single arm pulls using a lane rope to help simulate bent arm pull technique	pull through your body line	waves	3 mins
Repeat any previous drills using hand paddles	pull through to the thigh	waves	3 mins
2 lengths full stroke backstroke	continuous flowing strokes	waves	3 mins
Contrasting Activity: feet first sculling	feet remain at the surface	waves	3 mins
basic racing start	head tucked down on entry	one at a time	3 mins
Exit: using the pool steps or over the poolside	take your time	waves	1 min

Total time: 29 minutes

Lesson #12 Assessment

Lesson Objective: to develop and fine-tune backstroke arm action.		
Below average	**Average**	**Above average**
😐	🙂	😎
Attempts to demonstrate but does not show the correct technique	Able to perform most of the technique correctly some of the time	Performs the technique correctly most of the time

Assessment	😐	🙂	😎
Arm pulls are continuous and alternating			
Hand enters the water little finger first			
Fingers are together			
Arms are straight on entry			
Hand enters the water inline with the shoulder			

Lesson Plan #13

Lesson type: backstroke breathing
Level: adult or child beginner
Previous learning: basic back paddle
Lesson aim: to learn basic backstroke breathing technique
Equipment: floats, kickboards and buoyancy aids as necessary

Exercise/Activity	Teaching Points	Organisation	Duration
Entry: pool steps or swivel entry	enter slowly	all together	1 min
Warm up: 2 widths any stroke using buoyancy aids	take your time	all together	2 mins
Main Theme: kicking supine with a woggle under the arms	relax and breathe	all together	2 mins
supine push and glide, holding floats if needed	breathe out as you push off	waves	3 mins
supine kicking with a float held on the chest	continuous breathing	waves	3 mins
single arm pulls with a float held on the chest	breathe out as you pull	waves	3 mins
single arm pulls using the opposite arm with a float held on the chest	breathe out as you pull	waves	3 mins
2 widths full stroke backstroke	steady continuous breathing	waves	3 mins
Contrasting Activity: pencil jump	jump away from the side	all together	2 mins
tuck float (timed)	deep breath, chin to chest	all together	2 mins
Exit: using the pool steps	take your time	one by one	1 min

Total time: 26 minutes

Lesson #13 Assessment

Lesson Objective: to introduce basic backstroke breathing technique.		
Below average	**Average**	**Above average**
😐	🙂	😎
Attempts to demonstrate but does not show the correct technique	Able to perform most of the technique correctly some of the time	Performs the technique correctly most of the time

Assessment	😐	🙂	😎
Breathing is continuous			
Breathing is relaxed and unlabored*			

*allowances should be made for a swimmer's fitness and stamina levels, as these will affect breathing pattern and continuity.

Lesson Plan #14

Lesson type: backstroke breathing

Level: adult or child intermediate
Previous learning: basic backstroke technique
Lesson aim: to develop breathing technique while performing the full stroke
Equipment: floats, buoyancy aids and hoop

Exercise/Activity	Teaching Points	Organisation	Duration
Entry: swivel entry	enter slowly	all together	1 min
Warm up: 2 widths any stroke	slow and gentle swim	all together	3 mins
Main Theme: 2 widths full stroke backstroke	continuous arms and legs	waves	3 mins
supine push and glide from the poolside	breathe out slowly	waves	3 mins
kicking with float held on the chest	relaxed and steady	waves	3 mins
single arm pull, holding a float on the chest	exhale as you pull	waves	3 mins
repeat above exercise with the opposite arm	inhale as your arm recovers	waves	3 mins
full stroke, breathing in with one pull and out with the other	breathe in and out through your mouth	waves	3 mins
Contrasting Activity: push and glide through a submerged hoop	relax and stretch	2 or 3 at a time	3 mins
treading water for 60 seconds	mouth and nose out of the water	all together	2 mins
Exit: using the pool steps or over the poolside	take your time	one by one/all together	1 min

Total time: 28 minutes

110

Lesson #14 Assessment

Lesson Objective: to develop and progress basic backstroke breathing technique.		
Below average	**Average**	**Above average**
😐	🙂	😎
Attempts to demonstrate but does not show the correct technique	Able to perform most of the technique correctly some of the time	Performs the technique correctly most of the time

Assessment	😐	🙂	😎
Breathing is continuous			
Breathing is relaxed and unlabored*			
Breathing in and out follows arm cycles			

*allowances should be made for a swimmer's fitness and stamina levels, as these will affect breathing pattern and continuity.

Lesson Plan #15

Lesson type: backstroke breathing

Level: adult or child advanced
Previous learning: full stroke backstroke
Lesson aim: to develop and perfect backstroke breathing technique
Equipment: floats and/or kickboard if needed

Exercise/Activity	Teaching Points	Organisation	Duration
Entry: sitting or shallow dive entry	take your time	waves	1 min
Warm up: 2 lengths any stroke	take your time	all together	3 mins
Main Theme: 2 lengths full stroke backstroke	steady breathing	waves	2 mins
supine push and glide with arms extended	exhale as you glide	waves	3 mins
supine kicking with arms extended	breathe out slowly	waves	3 mins
single arm pulls using a lane rope to help simulate bent arm pull technique	pull and blow	waves	3 mins
2 lengths full stroke backstroke with steady rhythmical breathing	exhale as one arm pulls, inhale as the opposite arm pulls	waves	3 mins
2 lengths full stroke backstroke	continuous rhythmical breathing	waves	3 mins
Contrasting Activity: treading water - vary with 1 arm behind the back or above the water	ears and mouth above the surface	waves	3 mins
basic racing start	push hard from the legs	waves	3 mins
Exit: using the pool steps or over the poolside	take your time	one by one	1 min

Total time: 29 minutes

Lesson #15 Assessment

Lesson Objective: to develop and perfect backstroke breathing technique.

Below average	Average	Above average
😐	🙂	😎
Attempts to demonstrate but does not show the correct technique	Able to perform most of the technique correctly some of the time	Performs the technique correctly most of the time

Assessment	😐	🙂	😎
Breathing is continuous			
Breathing is relaxed and unlabored*			
Inhalation takes place as one arm pulls			
Exhalation takes place as opposite are pulls			
Breathing is continuous and rhythmical			

*allowances should be made for a swimmer's fitness and stamina levels, as these will affect breathing pattern and continuity.

Lesson Plan #16

Lesson type: backstroke timing and coordination
Level: adult or child beginner
Previous learning: basic back paddle and backstroke arm movement
Lesson aim: to learn basic coordination of arms and legs for backstroke
Equipment: floats, buoyancy aids and sinkers as necessary

Exercise/Activity	Teaching Points	Organisation	Duration
Entry: swivel entry	enter slowly	all together	1 min
Warm up: 2 widths any stroke using buoyancy aids	slow and gentle swim	all together	3 mins
Main Theme: 2 widths back paddle, using arms and legs	continuous kicking	waves	3 mins
supine push and glide adding leg kicks	count 3 kicks at a time	waves	3 mins
single arm pull, holding a float on the chest	3 kicks per arm pull	waves	3 mins
repeat above exercise with the opposite arm	count to 3 with each arm pull	waves	3 mins
push and glide adding arm pulls	continuous arms	waves	3 mins
full stroke, 3 kicks for each arm pull	continuous kicking as you pull	waves	3 mins
Contrasting Activity: prone star float	deep breath and relax	all together	2 mins
submerge to collect an object	eyes open	2 or 3 at a time	3 mins
Exit: using the pool steps or over the poolside	take your time	one by one	1 min

Total time: 28minutes

Lesson #16 Assessment

Lesson Objective: to introduce a basic backstroke timing pattern.		
Below average	**Average**	**Above average**
😐	🙂	😎
Attempts to demonstrate but does not show the correct technique	**Able to perform most of the technique correctly some of the time**	**Performs the technique correctly most of the time**

Assessment	😐	🙂	😎
Leg kicks are alternating			
Arm pulls are alternating			
Arms pulls and leg kicks balance each other			

Lesson Plan #17

Lesson type: backstroke timing and coordination

Level: adult or child intermediate
Previous learning: basic timing technique
Lesson aim: to progress and develop previous learning of backstroke timing
Equipment: floats if needed and hoop

Exercise/Activity	Teaching Points	Organisation	Duration
Entry: swivel or sitting dive entry	enter slowly	waves/ all together	1 min
Warm up: 2 widths any stroke	take your time	all together	3 mins
Main Theme: 2 widths full stroke backstroke	count 3 kicks at a time	all together	2 mins
single arm pull, holding a float on the chest	3 kicks per arm pull	waves	3 mins
repeat above exercise with the opposite arm	count to 3 with each arm pull	waves	3 mins
push and glide adding leg kicks	count 3 kicks at a time	waves	3 mins
backstroke catch-up (arms extended, one pull at a time)	maintain a kick and pull rhythm	waves	3 mins
full stroke, 3 kicks for each arm pull	continuous kicking as you pull	waves	3 mins
Contrasting Activity: feet first surface dives through a submerged hoop	stretch up and sink	one by one	4 mins
feet first sculling	toes at the surface	waves	3 mins
Exit: using the pool steps	take your time	one by one	1 min

Total time: 29 minutes

Lesson #17 Assessment

Lesson Objective: to progress and develop previous learning of backstroke timing.		
Below average	**Average**	**Above average**
😐	🙂	😎
Attempts to demonstrate but does not show the correct technique	Able to perform most of the technique correctly some of the time	Performs the technique correctly most of the time

Assessment	😐	🙂	😎
Leg kicks are alternating			
Arm pulls are alternating			
Arms pulls and leg kicks balance each other			
Timing is regular and rhythmical			

Lesson Plan #18

Lesson type: backstroke timing and coordination
Level: adult or child advanced
Previous learning: full stroke backstroke
Lesson aim: to develop and fine-tune backstroke timing
Equipment: floats and sinkers if needed, fins

Exercise/Activity	Teaching Points	Organisation	Duration
Entry: sitting or shallow dive entry	take your time	waves	1 min
Warm up: 2 lengths any stroke	take your time	all together	3 mins
Main Theme: 1 length full stroke backstroke	slow and steady	all together	2 mins
using fins, swim slow motion backstroke	smooth flowing movements	waves	3 mins
using fins, steady pace backstroke	let the legs balance the arms	waves	3 mins
arm pulls with pull buoy between the legs	continuous arms	waves	3 mins
push and glide, add arm pulls and leg kicks	continuous kicking	waves	3 mins
full stroke backstroke, 3 kicks for each arm pull	smooth and balanced	waves	3 mins
Contrasting Activity: head first surface dive and swim underwater for a pre-set distance	deep breath and dig down deep	one by one	3 mins
basic grab start	fast transition to stroke	waves	3 mins
Exit: using the pool steps	take your time	one by one	1 min

Total time: 28 minutes

Lesson #18 Assessment

Lesson Objective: to develop and fine-tune backstroke timing.		
Below average	**Average**	**Above average**
😐	🙂	😎
Attempts to demonstrate but does not show the correct technique	Able to perform most of the technique correctly some of the time	Performs the technique correctly most of the time

Assessment	😐	🙂	😎
Leg kicks are continuous and alternating			
Arm pulls are continuous and alternating			
Arms pulls and leg kicks balance each other			
Timing is regular and rhythmical			

"Now that you have finished my book, would you please consider writing a review? Reviews are the best way readers discover great new books. I would truly appreciate it."

Mark Young

For more information about teaching swimming, learning to swim and improving swimming technique visit **Swim Teach**.

Swim Teach
Teaching · Learning · Achieving · Professional Swimming Help Online

"The number one resource for learning to swim
and improving swimming technique."

www.swim-teach.com

www.ingramcontent.com/pod-product-compliance
Lightning Source LLC
Chambersburg PA
CBHW062047090426
42740CB00016B/3052